Blue Hitı

Chelsea's 25 Greatest Goals

Paul Radcliffe

Blue Hitmen
Chelsea's 25 Greatest Goals
Copyright Paul Radcliffe 2020
ISBN: 979-8457295704

Cover design: James Smith @jamessmithdesign (Instagram)
www.gate17.co.uk

CONTENTS

ACKNOWLEDGEMENTS

Thanks must go to the brilliant team of national press football writers whose contemporaneous reports I have used to check facts and correct my memories of individual matches. I would also like to thank all the former players and pundits who gave their time so generously recalling games from many years ago. Special thanks to my friend Peter 'Rosie' Rhoades-Brown for his advice and packed contact book. Finally, I would like to thank Mark Worrall at Gate 17 for his guidance and patience in the production of this book and Tim Rolls for proofreading it.

BLUE HITMEN

For Jamie

FOREWORD

AS a goal-scorer I was intrigued to be asked to write a few words for this book listing Chelsea's 25 greatest goals. Supporters love goals and the thrill of scoring was what kept me hungry for success throughout my career.

Some Chelsea fans have computer-like memories and can tell you who scored the goals against so-and-so on a wet Wednesday night, over 35 years ago.

Then there are the special goals, the goals that stay with you forever. An individual moment of genius indelibly printed in your memory bank, a goal that in decades to come will make you proud to have been there to witness it.

Alternatively, it may be a deflection or a cross that a player manages to knock in with his ear, it's the moment and the context that's important. Ask David Webb.

What are the circumstances? Was it a last-minute winner, did Chelsea need the victory for promotion or a trophy, was it the vital goal against our bitter rivals? Or, as in Chelsea's case, was the existence of our football club at stake?

When I was lucky enough to play for the Blues I remember us scoring specifically for our fans, for their amazing support. In the old Division Two we were 3-0 down at Cardiff City and struck back to draw 3-3, roared on by the 7,000 Chelsea supporters who had made the journey.

Likewise, at Hillsborough in the Milk Cup Quarter-final we were 3-0 down to Sheffield Wednesday but could hear the Chelsea fans singing defiantly at half-time. We fought back to 4-4, winning the replay.

Then there are the big game goals, the crucial clashes, the Cup Finals and European encounters that live in the collective memory at a football club.

Who could forget the contribution of our superstars including Didier Drogba, Frank Lampard and Eden Hazard?

We now live in an era of instant replays from every angle and slow-motion analysis of goals. In the earlier decades of Chelsea's existence none of this was available so we don't have footage of many goals from George Hilsdon, Roy Bentley and even Jimmy Greaves. Hence the emphasis on the last 50 years.

The author Paul Radcliffe has been a Chelsea supporter all his life and hopes to have revived plenty of memories for fans to chat about in the pub.

Enjoy the read and look forward to more wonderful Chelsea goals to come.

Kerry Dixon
Blue Hitman!

AUTHOR'S NOTE

EVERY Chelsea fan has their own idea about the greatest goals scored by the Blues. A lot depends on your age and when you started coming to Stamford Bridge - or watching games on television.

My choice of 25 goals reflects my experience as a match going fan from the seventies to the present day, with a vital penalty from 1955 thrown in as well.

There are title and trophy winning goals which no Chelsea fan will ever forget plus some surprises and personal favourites including my last day as a single man – away at Old Trafford.

Many of my most enjoyable day-trips back in the eighties were the treks up north to the likes of Bolton and Barnsley, not just for the goals but for the atmosphere and Chels arriving in huge numbers.

I'm sure many of you will disagree with my choices, but have a read and come up with your own.

Apologies to all the great players who scored brilliant efforts that didn't make it into the book. Perhaps we should look at the top 100 next time?

Paul Radcliffe
London 2021

GOAL 25
Meireles screamer silences Benfica

UEFA CL Quarter-final, Chelsea 2-1 Benfica.
(First-leg 0-1. Chelsea win 3-1 on agg)
Wednesday, 04-04-2012 at Stamford Bridge.
Attendance, 37,264. Raul Meireles (90+2 mins)

Team: Petr Cech, Branislav Ivanovic, David Luiz, John Terry (Gary Cahill 59), Ashley Cole, John Obi Mikel, Frank Lampard, Ramires, Juan Mata (Raul Meireles 79), Salomon Kalou, Fernando Torres (Didier Drogba 88).

RAUL MEIRELES may seem an unlikely contender in this book of pivotal goals for Chelsea, but if you cast your mind back to the 2011-12 Champions League campaign he scored an absolute screamer.

After overcoming Napoli in the last sixteen Chelsea faced Benfica in the quarter-finals.

David Luiz said, 'We are two good teams and there is pressure for both sets of supporters. Benfica's fans are very passionate, especially at home, but we have the experience to deal with that.'

In the away game Chelsea defended well, created chances and won the tie with a second-half Salomon Kalou goal.

Petr Cech made several decisive saves and the Blues survived a penalty appeal for handball by John Terry. Juan Mata hit the post and came close again later in the second-half but this time one goal was enough to give us victory.

Meireles and John Obi Mikel were the deeper midfielders and Fernando Torres played up-front while David Luiz replaced Gary Cahill in the centre of defence. Toward the end of the first half Benfica began to establish control, they were pressing high and Bruno Cesar had some long-range chances. After the break the gentle pace of the first-half was forgotten as Benfica turned up the pressure.

John Terry had dealt well with a series of crosses and shots but Benfica were outraged when the ball hit his arm in the penalty area but nothing was given by Italian referee Paolo Tagliavento.

In the 74th minute Ramires played in Torres down the right and the centre forward turned goal-maker by picking out Kalou for a close-range finish.

Meireles, who had been substituted for Frank Lampard in the 64th minute, received a hostile barrage of whistles and jeers as he walked from the pitch because of his long association with Benfica's bitter rivals Porto.

This was to come back to haunt the fans from the Estadio da Luz the following week at Stamford Bridge.

Manager Roberto Di Matteo said, 'We looked solid defensively, well organised and I always fancied us to score a goal. We're pleased we are in a different position going into the next leg. We had a had a mountain to climb against Napoli… this will be a bit smaller. But it's not a result you can rely on for the home game.'

He was right. Benfica made a high-tempo start, attacking The Shed End containing their fans, in search of an away goal. Lampard and Terry both made important blocks on the edge of the area before the Blues eventually got the ball into the opposition half.

Chelsea were catching Benfica on the break and the Slovenian referee gave Oscar Cardozo a yellow card for a heavy challenge on David Luiz. A minute later the referee awarded a penalty as Ashley Cole was bundled over in the area. Bruno Cesar and Maxi Pereira were both booked for dissent.

Lampard put the Blues ahead with the spot-kick into the bottom corner for his 22nd UEFA Champions League goal. It was 2-0 on aggregate with only 20 minutes played.

The cards kept coming with yellows for Branislav Ivanovic and Ramires, but Pereira's studs-up challenge on John Obi Mikel earned him his second yellow of the evening before half-time and he trudged forlornly down the tunnel.

After the break a second Chelsea goal looked like it was coming but Ramires ended up in the net rather than the ball. Torres looked to have placed a shot inside the post but a tiny deflection took it just wide.

Chelsea's grip on the match faded slightly as Benfica kept their shape and in the 84th minute a flicked header from unmarked Javi Garcia made it 1-1 to set nerves jangling around The Bridge.

However, a fantastic run from his own half by substitute Raul Meireles, supported by Ramires, stretched the depleted backline even further. Inside stoppage time the Portuguese international, who had been booed all night by the Benfica fans, hit a scintillating angled-shot to beat the keeper.

After the game Lampard said, 'We were sitting on a result so you don't want to go gung-ho, but we created enough chances in the second half to wrap it up without dominating the game.'

Manager Di Matteo said, 'I said at half-time that we needed that second goal to kill the game off. Every time you don't do that you know it's going to be hard work until the ref blows the final whistle.'

And Mata added, 'We are in the semi-finals and it is a gift for us to be there. Barcelona have most of the best players in the world but we are Chelsea and we will fight. Are they beatable? In football nothing is impossible. Of course, it will be difficult. They can play just as well away as at home, but we will see.'

Courtesy of Meireles' magnificent strike Chelsea were through to another Champions League semi-final, this time against reigning champions FC Barcelona.

Meireles came to Chelsea in August 2011 when the club was in the market for a midfielder following a long-term injury to Michael Essien. He signed on a four-year deal for an undisclosed fee reported to be in the region of £12 million. He chose the squad number 16 due to the fact he often wore it when on international duty.

He later said the chance to work with Andre Villas-Boas, with whom he had spent a short period of time at Porto, was too good an opportunity to turn down.

Meireles made his debut in September 2011 against Sunderland, which ended in a 2-1 away win with him setting up Daniel Sturridge's goal with a long pass.

In the following month, he scored his first goal for the club during a Champions League group stage 5-0 victory over KRC Genk. Meireles netted for the first time in the domestic League to contribute to a 2-1 home win against League leaders Manchester City at Stamford Bridge.

Meireles scored a goal and provided two assists to Torres, who ended his goal drought in the 5-2 home triumph against Leicester City in March 2012 for the quarter-finals of the FA Cup.

He won his first trophy in English football after a 2-1 win against his former club Liverpool in the FA Cup Final where he replaced Ramires for the last 15 minutes.

The Portuguese sat out the Champions League Final against FC Bayern Munich after receiving a yellow card against Barcelona at Camp Nou, but was still given a medal for his participation after the 4-3 victory on penalties.

Chelsea faced Benfica again just a year later on May 15, 2013 in the UEFA Europa League Final in front of a crowd of 46,163 at the Amsterdam Arena, the home of Ajax since 1996.

Both clubs had finished third in their Champions League groups and entered the Europa League in the round of 32.

To reach the final Chelsea overcame, on aggregate, the Czech Republic's Sparta Prague 2-1 in the last 32; Romania's Steaua Bucharest 3-2 in the last 16; Russia's Rubin Kazan 5-4 in the quarter-final and Switzerland's Basel 5-2 in the semi-final.

Chelsea captain Terry missed the game through injury and Belgian Eden Hazard was also absent after picking up a hamstring injury during the Blues' Premier League victory over Aston Villa on May 11.

Three players faced their former clubs in the final, David Luiz and Ramires were transferred from Benfica to Chelsea, while Nemanja Matic was transferred from Chelsea to Benfica (before returning to Chelsea again in 2014).

The game was a tight affair but Torres broke the deadlock midway through the second half, rounding the 'keeper and clipping in after being put through on goal by Juan Mata after 60 minutes, to the delight of an enormous Chelsea contingent of travelling fans.

Just eight minutes later the referee awarded a penalty after an Eduardo Salvio header struck Cesar Azpilicueta's hand. Oscar Cardozo hit home from the penalty spot.

The game looked to be heading for extra-time when three minutes into time added on Branislav Ivanovic climbed high to score from a looping header into the far corner of the net. The strike clinched a late but deserved 2-1 victory for the Blues and with it their first Europa League title.

Benfica had to reflect on a seventh successive defeat in a European final while Chelsea tried to make sense of a season rife with controversy, much of it regarding manager Rafael Benitez, but once again one finishing on a high.

Chelsea also became one of only five teams who have won the four major UEFA trophies, Champions League (2012), Europa League (2013, 2019), Cup Winners Cup (1971, 1998) Super Cup (1998). The other teams are Ajax, Bayern Munich, Juventus and Manchester United.

GOAL 24
Ashley celebrates eight goal title party

Premier League. Chelsea 8-0 Wigan Athletic.

Sunday, 09-05-2010 at Stamford Bridge.

Attendance, 41,383. Ashley Cole (90)

Team: Petr Cech, Branislav Ivanovic (Juliano Belletti 58), Ashley Cole, John Terry, Alex, Frank Lampard, Michael Ballack (Nemanja Matic 70), Florent Malouda, Didier Drogba, Solomon Kalou (Joe Cole 58), Nicolas Anelka.

CHELSEA recaptured the Premier League title in emphatic style as Ashley Cole volleyed home in the final minute to complete an 8-0 thrashing of Wigan Athletic.

Carlo Ancelotti's side needed a win to end Manchester United's three-year reign and after Nicolas Anelka gave them a sixth minute lead the game became a procession for Chelsea's scorers.

Chelsea had put seven past Sunderland, Aston Villa and Stoke City in the season but they celebrated by going one better against Roberto Martinez's side.

The win is the biggest domestic triumph in their history and they also scored the most League goals in a Premier League Season – 103.

The Blues broke the deadlock when an arguably offside Florent Malouda cushioned the ball to Nicolas Anelka, who clipped it home at 'keeper Mike Pollitt's near post.

Despite Wigan enjoying a fair share of possession and territory Chelsea scored their second goal after 32 minutes.

The eventual outcome was put beyond doubt when Gary Caldwell was sent off for hauling down Frank Lampard in the penalty area, the midfielder duly dusting himself down to bury the spot-kick.

However, this was much to the evident disappointment of Didier Drogba who wanted to bolster his claim for the Golden Boot.

Chelsea emerged early for the second half and went into a huddle before making their class pay in the race for the title.

In the 54th minute Salomon Kalou banished any lingering doubts among the fans when he exchanged passes with Lampard before beating Pollitt. Two minutes later Anelka hit a perfect right-foot volley from Branislav Ivanovic's cross to make it 4-0 and send Stamford Bridge into ecstasy.

With the title now heading for West London the only remaining issue to be worked on was Drogba's hunt for the Golden boot.

That was settled in the 63rd minute when the Ivorian rose highest at the far post to head Lampard's cross and see it nestle into the back of the net making it 5-0, the 100th goal of the season.

It got better for Drogba five minutes later when Ashley Cole was brought down by Mario Melchiot and Lampard tossed the ball to Drogba so he could take the penalty.

Lampard stood aside as Drogba's strike went in off the post but it mattered little to the Ivorian who had taken his tally for the season in the League to 28 and the score to 6-0.

Ancelotti was loudly acclaimed by Chelsea fans throughout the second half – and let his normally impassive mask slip with a fierce clenched-fist salute to a euphoric Stamford Bridge.

Drogba completed his hat-trick ten minutes from the end of the game as Chelsea made it seven in a match for the fourth time in the season.

Substitute Joe Cole's shot was parried by Pollitt but the ball fell kindly to Drogba who tucked it home for goal number 29.

The goal sparked more rapturous appreciation for Ancelotti but Wigan, who had not tested Petr Cech at all during the one-sided contest, finally forced him into action when the big Czech 'keeper tipped a goal-bound shot from Victor Moses over the bar in the 87th minute.

If the cake required a cherry on top, Ashley Cole provided it with a beautiful low finish past the shell-shocked Pollitt, before joyous scenes engulfed Stamford Bridge when referee Martin Atkinson blew the final whistle.

Captain John Terry said he hadn't slept the night before the match and he was more nervous than he had ever felt before.

Chelsea had lost at the DW Stadium earlier in the season and another upset was always a possibility. However, Terry said, 'We went and smashed them 8-0. The nerves and excitement before these big, important, decisive games are really vital to me.'

Chelsea still had a potential League and cup double to play for with the FA Cup Final against Portsmouth coming up in just six days.

With scenes of celebration going on all around Stamford Bridge, Terry said, 'Amazing. It's the first time a few of the lads have won the Premier League here. It's been three years since I won it and it's not a nice feeling. Today, this is what I remember, this is the feeling. This is what I want more of.'

Ashley Cole, scorer of Chelsea final goal, was also taking in every moment of the celebrations on the pitch. He said, 'I love Chelsea – I've been here years now – and I'd love to stay here as long as I can.'

Cole was born in Stepney, London, in December 1990. His father Ron Callender is from Barbados but later lived in England and then Australia. Cole was brought up by his mother Sue Cole going to Bow School and later Tower Hamlets.

Left-back Cole began his youth and professional career with North London club Arsenal before, after a protracted transfer saga, he completed a move to Stamford Bridge in August 2006.

He was given the No.3 shirt at Chelsea and made his first appearance for the club as a substitute for Wayne Bridge in their 2-1 win over Charlton Athletic in September, 2006.

Early in the New Year Cole suffered a serious knee injury in the 3-0 victory over Blackburn at Stamford Bridge. However, later scans revealed it was not quite as bad as originally thought and Chelsea were optimistic that he would return before the end of the season.

Cole did return at the end of the season, playing in the last twelve minutes of the 2007 FA Cup Final at the new Wembley Stadium against Manchester United. Chelsea emerged victorious 1-0 after extra-time with a goal scored by Didier Drogba.

Cole scored his first Chelsea goal, the fourth in a 4-0 away victory over West Ham United in March, 2008.

The following season after starting Chelsea's first six games in the League, Cole scored his third, fourth and fifth Chelsea goals in games at home to Burnley, Tottenham Hotspur and Sunderland respectively.

In September 2009 he signed a new four-year deal which contracted him to Chelsea until 2013. However, in February 2010 he suffered a fractured left ankle in a game against Everton that kept him out of action for three months. He eventually made his return in a match against Stoke which Chelsea won 7-0.

After his powerful goal in the 8-0 defeat of Wigan, Cole then played in the 2010 FA Cup Final victory over Portsmouth to give him the second League and cup double of his career.

He started all 38 games for Chelsea in the 2010-11 season and was awarded the Chelsea FC Players' Player of the Year award for the second time.

England international Cole won his seventh FA Cup final in Chelsea's 2-1 victory over Liverpool in 2012.

In the Champions League semi-final against Barcelona, Cole was pivotal in Chelsea's 1-0 victory which included a goal-line clearance that denied Barca an away goal. He also received praise for his role in the final against Bayern Munich on 19 May, 2012, both for his defending and for scoring in the decisive penalty shoot-out as Chelsea won their first European Cup.

Cole scored his first goal for over two years in a 1-0 victory against an obdurate Stoke side at Stamford Bridge in September, 2012. He made his 350th Premier League appearance in a defeat at West Ham in December, 2012.

In January 2013 Cole signed a one-year extension to his contract with

Chelsea. He again helped the club win a European trophy during the 2012-13 season playing in a 2-1 victory over Benfica in the UEFA Europa League Final in May.

Cesar Azpilicueta replaced Cole as Chelsea's first choice left-back in November 2013. Cole captained Chelsea for the last match of the season at Cardiff City on Sunday, 11 May, 2014.

He led the Blues to a 2-1 win with goals from Andre Schurrle and Fernando Torres. Cole's last appearance in a Chelsea shirt.

Reflecting on his career Cole said, 'People talk about my private life more than asking if I'm good at football. But they don't know me. Know me as a footballer.

'In football you can't always have it your own way. You can't always have the good times. You are going to have bad spells and periods when you are not playing well. It is something I have learned to deal with.'

Carlo Ancelotti won the double for Chelsea in his first season in English football and managed Cole at the peak of his career.

The following season saw Ancelotti axed by Roman Abramovich but Cole wanted to show his gratitude to the Italian boss.

Ancelotti said, 'On the bus coming home from my last game the players knew I was sacked and Ashley Cole said we must go out. I said no because we had ten friends visiting. We were going to have dinner at my house.

But Ashley said, 'No, no, they must all come I will send you a bus'. So, he sent a minibus to get us. It was unforgettable.'

GOAL 23
Fireworks as James seals comeback

UEFA Champions League. Chelsea 4-4 Ajax.

Wednesday, 05-11-2019 at Stamford Bridge.

Attendance, 39,132. Reece James (74)

Team: Kepa Arrizabalaga, Cesar Azpilicueta, Kurt Zuma, Fikayo Tomori, Marcus Alonso (Reece James 46), Mateo Kovacic (Michy Batshuayi 87), Jorginho, Mason Mount (Callum Hudson-Odoi 60), Willian, Tammy Abraham, Christian Pulisic.

THERE were eight goals, two of them own goals, two more ruled out by the video assistant referee, two red cards and two penalties in a night to thrill the denizens of Stamford Bridge.

Reece James, on for Marcus Alonso, hit Chelsea's fourth on Bonfire Night to make it 4-4 and earn a crucial Champions League point after the Blues had trailed 4-1.

The Dutch champions looked on course for victory when Donny van de Beek gave them a three-goal lead ten minutes after half-time – but in a chaotic closing period Chelsea completed a remarkable comeback as the visitors lost their discipline.

Having pulled one back through Cesar Azpilicueta's close-range finish to make it 4-2, the game turned on its head during 60 seconds of drama in the 68th minute.

Daley Blind fouled Chelsea's Tammy Abraham, referee Gianluca Rocchi allowed play to continue and a shot hit Joel Veltman's arm in the penalty area. Rocchi pointed to the spot, he then went back and showed Blind a second yellow card, with fellow centre-back Veltman also sent off seconds later for the handball.

Jorginho stepped forward to coolly convert from the spot for the

18

second time in the game to make it 4-3 and set up a frantic finale.

Ajax, so slick and clinical in the first half, were suddenly outnumbered and completely rattled.

The momentum had swung and substitute James levelled when he drove the ball into the net after Kurt Zouma headed against the bar from a corner.

James became the Blues' youngest ever Champions League goal-scorer, 19 years, 332 days, but there was no time for statistics when there was a winner to be found.

With the hosts pushing for victory backed by a vociferous crowd, Azpilicueta thought he had scored their fifth goal, only for VAR to intervene and detect an innocuous handball from Abraham. It seemed harsh but so did the handball against Veltman.

Ajax probably deserved something from the game for their flair and dead-ball delivery in the first half and their determination to hang on with nine men, even though they certainly rode their luck.

Michy Batshuayi twice went close in the pulsating closing phases and was denied by a fabulous save by Andre Onana.

Chelsea could be satisfied with their spirited response but the Blues' euphoria had to be tempered by their fragility at the back against set pieces.

It was an ending to match the game's opening, which featured two goals in the first four minutes, Abraham flicking Quincey Promes' free-kick into his own net before Jorginho equalised with his first penalty after Christian Pulisic was fouled.

Ajax retook the lead when Promes headed in a brilliant cross from Hakim Ziyech, whose free kick from a tight angle led to the third goal as the ball came back off the post and went in after hitting Kepa Arrizabalaga in the face.

Van de Beek looked to have settled the matter after 55 minutes, finishing off from 12 yards when unmarked, only for Chelsea to rally in stunning style.

Chelsea manager, Frank Lampard, said, 'I can't explain the game.

For all the things we might analyse back, the madness of the game, we are here for entertainment I suppose and anyone who watched that has to say 'what a game of football'. Respect to Ajax, what a spectacle.

'I don't think I have been to a game like it, the two own goals were the story of the first half. I said at half-time it will be 3-3 or 4-4, we were so in the game.

'We looked dangerous and I felt we would build momentum. I'm not happy overall, this is the Champions League and we made too many mistakes.

'The biggest pleasure is the spirit the whole stadium showed. I can't give you much on the red cards, I didn't really see what they were for.

'At half-time I would have taken a draw for sure. Let's take it for what it was. I was expecting somewhere towards 10 minutes of added time, I'm not sure where four came from.'

Ajax manager, Erik ten Hag, was asked about the Veltman handball and red card, he said, 'It was handball but what can he do with his hand? It's no handball, no booking, but we have to accept it.

'I'm proud of this team, it was a magnificent development and we take it as a positive.

'Everyone will have the same opinion from the stands and from the television. We dictated and we are very bitter that one decision could change everything.'

However, James was delighted with his first Champions League goal.

'I was in the box and the ball dropped for me, I just smashed it, really,' he said.

Asked about his classy goal celebration he added, 'I've seen that a lot, with arms stretched in a knee slide, but I've never done it before.'

James was born in Redbridge, London in December 1999 and had two seasons at Queens Park Rangers from the age of six. He said, 'When you are young you just want to get into the team. You just play and I loved scoring goals.'

When he moved to Chelsea as an eight-year-old he was still a striker.

'Reece was a naturally good footballer even from an early age,' said his under-8 coach. However, by the age of 15 the coaching staff had decided his potential was as a right-back.

'It was frustrating because I wanted to be scoring goals,' he said, 'But as time passed, I began to understand.

'It was difficult because as a Chelsea fan I had always looked up to Didier Drogba and his goals.'

He has represented England from under-17 to under-21 level. In 2017 he was included in an under-20 squad for the Toulon Tournament. He started in the final as England defeated the Ivory Coast to retain their title.

James was part of the under-19 squad that won the 2017 UEFA European Under-19 Championship. He started in the semi-final against the Czech Republic.

He was included in the under-21 squad for the first time in October 2019 and made his debut during the 3-0 victory in Albania.

During the 2017-18 season he captained the Chelsea under-18s to win the FA Youth Cup and was named Academy Player of the Season.

He signed a new four-year contract with the club in June 2018. Later that month he joined Wigan Athletic on loan for the 2018-19 season.

James said, 'It was great playing in the Championship against club mates including Tammy and Mason who were also out on loan.

'Going up to Wigan took a little bit of getting used to, but once I got into the rhythm, I was fine.'

He played every game in the Championship season except one and made a huge impact with the fans during his time with the club.

In March 2019 he was selected in the 2018-19 Championship team of the season. He also won three awards at Wigan's end of season awards, including Player of the Year.

Wigan's then manager, Paul Cook, said, 'I'm not speaking about Reece James. I don't need to. He's player of the month every month, and he's man of the match almost every week. There's nothing else I can say about him. And he's as good a lad as he is a player.'

James has proved that he can take his opportunity in a competitive senior League. His performances in the north-west had helped him show he may deserve a place in the Chelsea first-team.

In September 2019, James made his first-team debut for Chelsea after returning from injury. He scored one goal and assisted in two goals in a 7-1 win over Grimsby Town in the third round of the League Cup.

'It was a proud moment for me and my family,' said James. 'I know it's going to be tough getting in the team at right-back and for every position. I need to work hard and focus on myself.

'The chance to play in the first-team for my boyhood club is a dream.

'The transition between the Leagues is huge. The Championship is more physical, but you can get away with more.

'In the Premier League the quality is higher because of the standard of the players. If you make a mistake, you will give away a goal.

'Playing under the manager, Frank Lampard, is great. He is a club legend and all the players look up to him.'

James signed a long-term contract extension with Chelsea in January 2020. He comes from a footballing family where his sister, Lauren, is also a professional footballer with Chelsea F.C. Women. But what about life outside the game?

'At home I play Fortnite, I enjoy R&B music and I listen to Stormzy,' he said.

GOAL 22
Hasselbaink rocket scorches United

Premier League. Manchester United 3-3 Chelsea.

Saturday, 23-09-2000 at Old Trafford.

Attendance, 67,568. Jimmy Floyd Hasselbaink (7)

Team: Carlo Cudicini, Christian Panucci, Marcel Desailly, Frank Leboeuf, Graeme Le Saux, Tore Andre Flo, Jody Morris, Roberto Di Matteo, Jon Harley (Mario Melchiot 46), Gianfranco Zola (Samuele Dalla Bona 83), Jimmy Floyd Hasselbaink (Winston Bogarde 86).

WHEN Saturday comes the day before you get married you really can't spend all day watching Chelsea at Old Trafford can you? Yes, of course you can.

An 11.30am kick off in Manchester meant crawling out of bed incredibly early and making my train from Euston with at least 43 seconds to spare. Mainly Chelsea fans drinking coffee, reading the papers and playing cards. A carriage of Cockney Reds making their regular long journey *home.*

A lacklustre start to the season had cost manager Gianluca Vialli his job just a month into the campaign, despite having won five trophies since he was appointed in February 1998. The last of the trophies came at the start of the season when the dominant Blues defeated Manchester United 2-0 in the Charity Shield. Goals from Jimmy Floyd Hasselbaink and Mario Melchiot gave Chelsea victory in the last ever club game at the old Wembley.

Claudio Ranieri took over the reins at Stamford Bridge and eventually the big success of the season was the effectiveness of club record signing Hasselbaink, who found the net 23 times in 35 Premiership games in a partnership with Italian legend Gianfranco Zola, who scored nine times.

Hasselbaink was born in March, 1972, in Suriname, a small country and one of the poorest on the north eastern coast of South America. It is defined by vast swathes of tropical rainforest, Dutch colonial architecture and a melting-pot culture.

On its Atlantic coast is the capital, Paramaribo, where palm gardens grow near Fort Zeelandia, a 17th century trading post. Paramaribo is also home to St. Peter and Paul Basilica, a towering wooden cathedral consecrated in 1885.

Hasselbaink and his family later moved to the Dutch city of Zaandam in the province of North Holland located on the river Zaan, just north of Amsterdam.

It was there he began playing football initially as a goalkeeper, later as a right winger and finally as a forward. He began his senior career with SC Telstar and AZ Alkmaar in Holland then Portuguese clubs Campomaiorense and Taca de Portugal.

He was signed by Leeds United for £2 million before the 1997-98 season where he became a top marksman and went on to win the Premier League Golden Boot award in 1999. He was sold on to Spanish club Atletico Madrid, then managed by Ranieri, for £10 million the same year.

Hasselbaink returned to England with Chelsea for a club record £15 million fee in May 2000 and was reunited with Ranieri. He once again led the scoring table in his first season and won his second Premier League Golden Boot.

He also played in the 2002 FA Cup final and helped the Blues to a career high and then club record second place Premier League finish in 2003-4. He moved to Middlesbrough on a free transfer in July 2004 before playing for Charlton Athletic and Cardiff City at the end of his playing career.

But on a beautiful morning in September, 2000 as sunlight slanted across the pitch at Old Trafford many of those exploits were still to come and Hasselbaink's days with Chelsea were in their infancy.

Both sides had ambitions for the title before the season began but Chelsea came to Old Trafford with just one League win in their first six matches to their name, a 4-2 victory over West Ham at Stamford Bridge.

For the early kick-off the two teams were meeting in the Premiership for the first time in the season. After four minutes Roy Keane tangled with Jody Morris in the centre and won a free-kick which was simply floated into the penalty area and cleared by Chelsea.

In Ranieri's first game in English football the Blues started brightly and took the lead through an unstoppable Hasselbaink strike from the wide-left edge of the penalty area after just seven minutes.

As United tried to repair the deficit David Beckham made a run down the left and struck a cross but it bypassed three red shirts in the penalty area. However, minutes later Paul Scholes scored to make it 1-1.

After 22 minutes Beckham was rushed from the pitch after suffering from a heavily-bleeding cut to the head after a collision with Graeme Le Saux. Eventually he came back on after being treated.

Good build up play from Chelsea after 33 minutes resulted in a fine ball being played out to Hasselbaink wide on the right but he was harshly judged to be offside.

After 36 minutes Teddy Sheringham was on hand to score as Andy Cole missed a through ball after Scholes had left Denis Irwin's pass.

Two minutes later Sheringham knocked on a ball from Cole as Chelsea were caught in possession. His shot came off the post into the path of Beckham who made no mistake.

Hasselbaink squared the ball for Tore Andre Flo after 43 minutes as Chelsea aimed to pull one back before the break but United cleared the danger.

However, in a topsy-turvy first half Le Saux strode down the left and despite almost running the ball too far, he was able to pull it back perfectly for Flo whose strike baffled the hapless 'keeper Raimond Van Der Gouw and hit the back of the net to make it 3-2 at half-time.

Chelsea make a bright start to the second half with some good possession as they aimed to pull back a one-goal deficit.

After 50 minutes Beckham launched a 50-yard cross-field ball which fell directly into the path of Ryan Giggs who forced a corner, but Chelsea once again won possession.

Chelsea began to win the battle of the midfield and Beckham was forced to concede a corner which was driven in just missing the head of Flo.

After 56 minutes a Zola free-kick on the right was turned goalwards by the head of Christian Pannuci but Van Der Gouw parried it and United took the ball upfield.

Two minutes later the match continued to produce end-to-end action as Hasselbaink had a half-chance but his shot soared above the bar.

On 60 minutes a crucial tackle from Marcel Desailly took the ball away from Sheringham while in space deep inside the Chelsea area with two red shirts to his left.

After 64 minutes Cole came forward and beat Desailly, his shot then beat 'keeper Carlo Cudicini, but unbelievable defensive work from Le Saux saw him track back and brilliantly clear the ball off the line for a corner. What an escape for the Blues.

And just five minutes later Chelsea were level. Le Saux produced a stunning run down the left, he beat Beckham and pulled back a cross which Zola was able to steer in to the path of Flo for the big Norwegian striker to score.

United found themselves on the back foot for the first time in the match and Chelsea found their way through time and time again as they looked for a winner.

Morris then fouled Sheringham in the centre circle but they both ended up being yellow carded after the United striker showed his frustration.

After 85 minutes Flo won Chelsea a corner taken by Morris but Hasselbaink's pass to Leboeuf was turned in to the side netting.

The minutes ticked away and the game finished in a 3-3 draw after Chelsea completed a tenacious fightback in the second half.

Hasselbaink's flying start to his Chelsea career developed nicely over his first two seasons with two sixth places finishes.

The following two seasons, though they weren't as personally productive for Hasselbaink, saw Chelsea finish fourth and second and saw him as part of a partnership with Eidur Gudjohnsen. The duo developed an excellent understanding on the pitch with the cool Scandinavian complementing the intense Dutchman.

There was also a Champions League semi-final appearance against AS Monaco after knocking out Arsenal's *Invincibles* with a memorable victory at Highbury.

In this period Roman Abramovich had taken over at Chelsea and the Blues were starting to spend big. Hernan Crespo and Adrian Mutu both arrived in deals from Serie A to bolster the forward line.

Ranieri described the latter as a 'shark' but Hasselbaink remained the deadliest predator at Stamford Bridge, outscoring both players in 2003-04 before he left for Middlesbrough at the start of the first Mourinho era.

Hasselbaink, always controversial, said, 'Under Mourinho I could have been a Premiership champion. I've not won many medals so I think of what might have been.'

After his wonderful strike at Old Trafford and many other classic goals he also responded to football pundits who allegedly said hitting the back of the net is as thrilling as life gets.

Hasselbaink said, 'You can never say a goal is better than sex – all the guys who are saying that are not having proper sex.'

And on that note after a memorable 3-3 draw your author set off for the train home to prepare for the following day's big fixture.

GOAL 21
Sillett makes Wolves pay huge penalty

League Division One. Chelsea 1 Wolverhampton Wanderers 0.
Saturday, 09-04-1955 at Stamford Bridge.
Attendance, 75,043. Peter Sillett 75 (pen)

Team: Charlie Thomson, Peter Sillett, Stan Willemse, Ken Armstrong, Stan Wicks, Derek Saunders, Eric Parsons, Johnnie McNichol, Roy Bentley, Seamus O'Connell, Frank Blunstone.

A DEADLY penalty from Peter Sillett put the Division One title within Chelsea's grasp in an enthralling game at a packed Stamford Bridge.

Chelsea dominated the game and Wolverhampton Wanderers' England keeper Bert Williams made great saves from Eric Parsons, Roy Bentley and Seamus O'Connell.

The match remained goalless until 15 minutes from the end when another shot from O'Connell's beat Williams and was punched away over the bar by England skipper Billy Wright. The penalty was hammered home by fullback Peter Sillett, calm and composed in front of a rapturous crowd of 75,043, with the gates closed before kick-off

Even then there was still some work to be do. A goalless draw against Portsmouth meant that a win over already relegated Sheffield Wednesday coupled with a Portsmouth failure to beat Cardiff City would guarantee the title with one game remaining.

Two goals from Parsons and another penalty from Sillett were enough to see off Wednesday. There was then an agonising wait to hear that Pompey had drawn and Chelsea were champions.

Sillett, 22, was a hard, uncompromising defender who feared no one. He was not particularly quick or an exceptional tackler but his mastery of full-back play and excellent passing ability meant he was an automatic choice for the next six seasons, barring a period out following a knee operation at the start of the '56 campaign. He came to Chelsea from Southampton, with his brother John, 16, at the start of the Championship season.

John who was watching the game said, 'It was an amazing time to have to take a penalty, but there couldn't have been a cooler man in the group than Peter.

'He had great force in his shot. Even to this day Peter had the most powerful shot I have ever seen. I was biting my nails as I sat in the stand but Peter wouldn't be rushed.

'He walked rather than ran towards the ball on the penalty spot then absolutely smashed it past Bert Williams. He was as cool as a cucumber. Just the man for the job.'

John went on to have an illustrious career, playing 102 games for Chelsea often alongside his brother, and going on to play for Coventry City and Plymouth Argyle. He then went into management taking Coventry to a 3-2 FA Cup Final victory over Tottenham Hotspur in 1987.

When he signed David Speedie from Chelsea he was quoted as saying, 'Coventry City have shopped at Woolworth's for too long, from now on we are shopping at Harrods.'

At the beginning of the jubilee season Chelsea had never won a trophy, but that all changed under manager Ted Drake who had been slowly improving the team. However, four consecutive defeats in October left them in mid-table with their Championship hopes fading. Then they embarked on a run of just three defeats in 23 games.

On Easter Saturday Chelsea entertained Wolverhampton Wanderers, their nearest rivals. It was likely to be a winner takes all contest for the Championship.

For some the club's success was unexpected, Chelsea had never won a major trophy before and their League position in recent seasons had ranged from eighth to twentieth.

Chelsea had beaten title rivals Wolves twice, the game at Molineux a 3-4 thriller (John McNichol, Bentley 2, Les Stubbs) to secure the

Championship with a game to spare. Club captain **Bentley** finished as top scorer, with 21 goals, and the club attracted an average home gate of 48,307, the highest in the division. At the time it was the club's most successful season ever.

Chelsea boss Drake was an English football player and manager who started his top flight career at Southampton before playing for Arsenal in the 1930s. He holds the record for the most goals scored in a senior game in English football, with seven against Aston Villa in December 1935.

A former **centre forward**, Drake has been described as a 'classic number 9' and as a 'strong, powerful, brave player' who typified the English approach.

Interestingly, Chelsea players feature strongly in the games with a high tally of goals for one man. George 'Gatling Gun' Hilsdon scored a double hat-trick in the club's 9-1 victory over Worksop in the FA Cup first round on January 11, 1908.

Five players have scored five goals in a match for Chelsea, Hilsdon, Jimmy Greaves (three times), Bobby Tambling, Peter Osgood and Gordon Durie.

Drake was appointed manager of Chelsea in 1952 without too much of a fanfare. His arrival saw him make a series of sweeping changes, doing much to rid the club of its previous amateurish, music hall image.

He discarded the club's famous Chelsea pensioner crest and with it the Pensioners nickname and insisted a new one be adopted. From these changes came the Lion Rampant Regardant crest and the Blues nickname.

He introduced scouting reports and a new, tougher, training regime based on ball work, a rare practice in English football at the time.

The club's previous policy of signing big-name players was abandoned, instead Drake used his knowledge of the lower divisions and the amateur game to recruit little-known, but often more reliable players. These included the Sillett brothers, McNichol and Frank Blunstone.

Within three years, in the 1954-55 season, Drake had led Chelsea to their first League Championship triumph. In doing so, he became the first person to win the League title both as player and manager.

However, Drake never came close to repeating the success. The Championship-winning side was gradually broken up, to be replaced by the crop of youngsters emerging from the club's youth team, such as Greaves, Peter Brabook and Tambling, for whom Drake was an aloof figure.

In the following seasons performances and results from the youngsters were often erratic, leaving the club stranded in mid-table. An FA Cup loss to Fourth Division Crewe Alexandra weakened Drake's position at the club and a few months later, he was sacked early into the 1961-62 season.

After leaving Chelsea, he became reserve team manager at Fulham, where he was also assistant to the manager Vic Buckingham. In December he joined Barcelona as assistant to Buckingham, staying until June 1970. He later returned to Fulham where he became a chief scout, director and life president of the Cottagers. Drake died at the age of 82 on 30 May 1995.

As Champions in 1955, Chelsea were entitled to a place in the newly launched European Cup but, sadly for the ebullient Drake, the League and the Football Association forbade entry and the Stamford Bridge board accepted the ruling.

Penalty scorer Sillett was a cultured distributor of the ball, his positional play was astute and he was exceptionally cool under pressure. However, it was as one of the most explosively powerful dead-ball kickers of his and any era that earns him most renown.

He was a menace anywhere within 40 yards of the opponents' goal and was the author of some of the most spectacular strikes ever seen at Stamford Bridge. In fact opponents often used to place defensive walls even when Sillett struck free kicks from almost the halfway line such was his power and accuracy.

Chelsea legend and captain of the 1954/5 Championship winning side, Roy Bentley said, 'Peter was one of the greatest passers of a ball I have ever seen and the first man in the game that could regularly produce 100 yard passes direct to a teammate.'

Sillett played the game rather like a Rolls Royce, there was nothing showy or flashy about him but his exceptional natural talent and quality shined through to the discerning observer and those within the game.

Technically superb Sillett was courted by Italian giants Juventus but turned down the move in typically laid back fashion by reportedly stating that Italy was 'too bloody hot for football'.

England and Wolves captain Wright once said to Sillett's brother, John, 'If I was a 100 cap player, then so was Peter.' In fact he only won three full England caps.

At one point Sillett was hotly tipped to be a captain of the England senior side but perhaps it was his cool, relaxed and modest attitude to both life and the game, allied to the fact that he was universally regarded as a notoriously poor trainer, which stopped him doing full justice to the huge talent which should have made him one of the giants of British football.

Sillett made a total of 288 appearances for Chelsea and remained at the club until June 1962, when new manager Tommy Docherty made a series of sweeping changes to the playing squad. Peter Sillett died at the age of 65 in 1998.

GOAL 20
King Canners takes comeback crown

Football League Cup, quarter-final replay.

Sheffield Wednesday 4-4 Chelsea.

Wednesday, 30-01-1985 at Hillsborough Stadium.

Attendance, 36,505. Paul Canoville (46, 85)

Team: Eddie Niedzwiecki, Joey Jones, Doug Rougvie, Colin Lee (Paul Canoville 46), Joe McLaughlin, Dale Jasper, Pat Nevin, Nigel Spackman, Kerry Dixon, David Speedie, Mickey Thomas.

SIX thousand Chelsea supporters travelled to Hillsborough Stadium on a bitterly cold night to help the Blues secure a win following a 1-1 draw in London two days earlier.

Unfortunately, Chelsea did not get off to a strong start. Howard Wilkinson's Sheffield Wednesday were up 3-0 at half-time, and our players were left frustrated

At the interval as the team regrouped the visiting Blues fans impressed the players by singing loudly and willing them to stay defiant, 'We are the famous, the famous Chelsea.'

Before manager John Neal's team talk, players including Joey Jones and Joe McLaughlin berated the team to get back out and fight one of Chelsea's greatest rivals of that era.

The high spirits in the stands helped get the team back into the game. Just 11 seconds after coming on as a substitute at the start of the second half, Paul Canoville, tapped in the first goal for the Blues.

Kerry Dixon squeezed in another at the 64th minute, fuelling the Chelsea hordes even more. The equalizer, on 76 minutes, was a wonderful shot by winger Mickey Thomas into the top of the net from a distance, sending the massed Chelsea ranks into ecstasy.

The amazing vocal support went up another notch and after 85 minutes, that man Canoville tapped in another, nearly running over opposing 'keeper Martin Hodge. At 3-4 what had seemed like an unlikely victory was so close, but it would actually be days away.

In the final seconds of regular time, Wednesday's Mel Sterland was tripped by Doug Rougvie and scored via a penalty, making the score 4-4. With both teams exhausted, the game ended with honours even. It was a disappointing finish for both sides, but certainly a comeback to remember.

'If you talk to the supporters from that era, that 4-4 always gets mentioned. It was amazing,' confirmed midfielder Nigel Spackman. The draw forced a second replay, this time at Stamford Bridge, a hard-fought 2-1 win for John Neal's side.

Looking back on the match Canoville said, 'It really made me realise what great support we had. Wherever we played, whenever we played there would be thousands of supporters with us. Our fans were our number 12.'

However, to get to that point Canoville - the first black player in Chelsea's first-team - had endured years of abuse on and off the pitch in one of the most extreme examples of racism in football in the eighties.

Paul Kenneth Canoville was born in Southall, Middlesex to Udine Patricia 'Patsy' Lake in March, 1962. His mother emigrated to England from Anguilla in the Leeward Islands, a British overseas territory in the Caribbean.

Patsy raised him and his sister June alone as his father had no interest in raising a family. Udine was one of the Windrush generation from the West Indies and ran a strict household working as a nurse and expecting good behaviour and aspiration from her children.

Canoville said, 'I knew at the age of five that I wanted to be a professional footballer, but as I grew up it was difficult for my mum to understand. Life in England was so different for her and she didn't see how football could be my job.'

The young Canoville wasn't academic but at school he played basketball, cricket, football and enjoyed athletics.

Canoville said, 'Mum never came to my games. Everybody wants a parent to say 'well done' or get excited when the local paper says you are an up and coming talent. Perhaps what I needed was a father, a mentor or brother?'

As a teenager he played truant from school and was sentenced to three months in borstal after he became involved in petty crime with the 'wrong sort' of friends. He needed some sort of discipline in his life and it acted as a wake-up call.

One person who did help him was Stephanie Caton, his mum's friend from church in Southall.

Canoville said, 'Auntie Stephanie was a rock and always calm and straightforward about things. She was there when I was sentenced by the magistrate.'

She said, 'You know, Paul, you want to be a professional footballer. But if you keep on like this, you're going to wind up at Her Majesty's Pleasure, not Wembley Stadium, and you won't be able to play no football.'

However, when his mother moved to Slough in 1979, Canoville slept rough and in hostels. He started playing semi-professionally for Southern League side Hillingdon Borough and slept in an abandoned car as he had nowhere to stay.

At Borough he was moved from centre-half to the wings, where his pace was a greater asset. He also managed to upgrade from a pair of boots his mother had bought for him in Woolworths to a pair of classy Puma Kings.

After two successful seasons with the club he had trials with Southampton, West Brom and Chelsea.

He signed for Neal's Chelsea in December 1981; he was paid £175 a week and Borough received a £5,000 fee.

'It was a dream come true. I really couldn't believe it was happening,' said Canoville. 'With my first pay packet from Chelsea I went down to

Harrods in Knightsbridge, London and casually bought myself a beautiful, £700 leather jacket.'

He made his debut against Crystal Palace at Selhurst Park in April, 1982, coming on as a late substitute for Clive Walker who had scored the only goal of the game.

Canoville said, 'As I completed my running and stretches I could hear vile abuse and racial taunts. All the excitement about making my debut drained out of me.

'I snatched a glimpse and realised the jeers were coming from people wearing blue shirts and scarves, our own fans with faces full of hate. I felt physically sick. I was absolutely terrified. I just didn't want to go on, it hit me so hard.

'Then I thought 'No', I'm not going to allow this to stop me becoming a professional footballer. I played for the last ten minutes and was just waiting for the referee's whistle to end the game.'

After the match in the dressing room there was none of the usual banter. It was very quiet. The manager said to me, 'Son, I can't begin to imagine how you felt. Show them your football.'

Canoville said, 'So that's what I did. I thought about playing elsewhere, but I stayed and fought. I look back to the 4-4 at Hillsborough as the moment when I really became part of Chelsea for my football not notable because of the colour of my skin.'

After the Palace game he ended the 1981-82 season with two late substitute appearances, replacing Peter Rhoades-Brown on the right-wing on both occasions.

He enjoyed a run of six games at the start of the 1982-83 season before he was sidelined with a thigh injury. He scored his first goal for the club with a volley in a 1-1 draw with Fulham.

With Chelsea facing relegation into the Third Division, Canoville was returned to the first-team and helped the club secure enough points to avoid the drop.

Scottish winger Pat Nevin was signed for the 1983-84 season and although they were rivals for the same position in the team they became good friends off the pitch. Nevin defended Canoville from the racist abuse he received during another game at Crystal Palace, two years after he had made his debut there.

The striker told the press after the match he didn't want to talk about his winning goal that took Chelsea into second place in the Second Division with six games to play.

'I'll never forget that Pat came out publicly and, as only Pat could, attacked those last few fans who were abusing me,' said Canoville.

Canoville had a good start to the season and scored a hat-trick against Swansea City in December. However, the next month Neal signed winger Mickey Thomas which reduced Canoville's first-team appearances.

Chelsea won promotion back to the First Division as champions of the Second Division and Canoville scored seven goals in 25 appearances.

He was in excellent form in the first half of the 1984 campaign but picked up an injury against Stoke City in December and started fewer games on recovery. He did however play a starring role in the League Cup tie at Sheffield Wednesday.

The Hillsborough game also had great personal significance for Canoville. His dad Vernon, who he hadn't seen for 21 years, lived in Sheffield and came along to meet his son in the Players' Bar after the match.

Canoville said, 'We started chatting, just light things. I didn't put him on the spot or ask him questions about the past. That is a period I can't do anything about.

'He asked me to come up and spend a longer time with him when I was freer, which I did. He's not much of a football fan, though. He never came to watch me play again.'

GOAL 19
Magic Mason casts spell over Madrid

UEFA Champions League, semi-final. Chelsea 2-0 Real Madrid.
(First-leg 1-1. Chelsea win 3-1 on agg)
Wednesday, 05-05-2021 at Stamford Bridge.
Behind closed doors. Mount (87)

Team: Edouard Mendy, Andreas Christensen, Thiago Silva, Toni Rudiger, Cesar Azpilicueta (Reece James 88), N'Golo Kante, Jorginho, Ben Chilwell, Mason Mount (Hakim Ziyech 89), Kai Havertz (Olivier Giroud 90+4), Timo Werner (Christian Pulisic 67)

A SUPERB Mason Mount goal three minutes from time put Chelsea through to the Champions League Final for the third time in their history.

On a night of high tension, even behind closed doors because of Covid restrictions, Chelsea fully deserved a victory that set up an all-English final against Manchester City, Pep Guardiola's Premier League Champions.

Timo Werner had put the Blues ahead on 28 minutes in a gutsy team performance full of passion and drive at Stamford Bridge.

Chelsea were grateful to 'keeper Edouard Mendy for two great first-half saves from Karim Benzema but they were able to build on the 1-1 draw they achieved in Madrid when Werner headed in from almost on the goal-line in the 28th minute after Kai Havertz had chipped on to the bar.

It set the pattern for a second half of Chelsea domination that was nevertheless nail biting as the hosts missed chance after chance to put the game to bed.

Real's ex-Chelsea 'keeper Thibaut Courtois saved from N'golo Kante and Havertz, who also headed against the bar, while Mount shot over the bar when clean through. It was Mount, though, who finally sealed Chelsea's place in their first Champions League final since they won the competition in 2012. The sublime Kante, who was also key in the opening goal, fed substitute Christian Pulisic who delayed his cross to pick out Mount who cleverly turned it in with just three minutes left on the clock.

After Chelsea's 2-0 win 22-year-old Mount said, 'I saw one of their players [Toni Kroos] had said he doesn't lose sleep over any of our players. Maybe he should lose sleep over us as a team.'

The hugely experienced German midfielder later responded on Twitter saying, 'Still sleeping ok. But well done yesterday, congrats.'

At the match itself rain in South-West London stopped just as the teams got underway. In early play there was a lively pace to the contest and a physical edge with Andreas Christensen challenging hard.

The classy Havertz was selected over Pulisic, the only change to the side that started in the draw played in torrential conditions at the Estadio Alfredo Di Stefano in Madrid the previous week.

Toni Rudiger wore a protective face mask after sustaining an injury in the first-leg. Another former Chelsea player, Eden Hazard, started for Madrid alongside Sergio Ramos and Ferland Mendy both coming back after injury.

Rudiger had the first Chelsea shot in anger, a long-range blast after 10 minutes, that Courtois had to punch away. Our former keeper then scrambled the ball away for a corner after Mount deftly danced into the box.

The midfield battle, as in the first-leg, was the key to controlling the game. In one swift move Mount, in space, found Ben Chilwell who delivered a low hard cross for Werner, fractionally offside, to convert.

The vital opening strike by Werner, whose work-rate has not been matched by goals this season, was a huge plus for Chelsea, as was the display of the improving Havertz, an elegant operator who was a constant threat.

Mendy played his part with those crucial interventions from Benzema, with Rudiger also a rock, but the home goalkeeper was virtually redundant after the break as Chelsea produced a wonderful display of skill and power.

Chelsea captain Cesar Azpilicueta, said, 'It was a massive performance for the team. We knew we had a tough opponent but we performed really well and could have scored more goals. In the second half we were clearly better.'

'We had to suffer but we fought really hard. We have one more step, we want to go to the Final to try to win it. For me, this is massive, we have plenty of things to fight for with some massive weeks coming up. We have played Manchester City a lot of times, but we believe in ourselves and are ready for it!'

In 2012 Chelsea won the Champions League Final on penalties after a 1-1 draw with Bayern Munich at the Allianz Arena in Munich. However, in 2008 after a 1-1 draw with Manchester United in Luzhniki Stadium in Moscow the Blues lost on penalties.

Tuchel stressed that for Chelsea's third final appearance in the competition, 'We will arrive with a clear focus to win the Champions League.'

Mount an attacking or central midfielder was born in Portsmouth, Hampshire, on January 10, 1999. He joined Chelsea's Academy in 2005 at the age of six and began his senior career on loan to Vitesse in the Dutch Eredivisie and Derby County in the Championship before making his Chelsea debut in 2019.

His father Tony was a player and manager at non-League local clubs such has Havant Town. Tony once said that despite the pressure of playing for the Chelsea Academy Mount still showed commitment to his education at Purbrook Park School in Waterlooville, north of Porstsmouth.

Mount was playing under-6 football in local Leagues as a four-year-old and later spent one day a week training in the academies of Chelsea and Portsmouth. He listed Frank Lampard, Luka Modric and Andres

Iniesta as his football role models.

He made his Chelsea under-18 debut as an under-15 during the 2013-14 season and added several more appearances in the following season. Mount went on to play for both the under-18 and under-21 teams during the 2016-17 season, in which he scored 10 goals in 30 appearances. He signed a new four-year contract with Chelsea in July 2017.

The youngster joined Dutch Eredivisie Club Vitesse in July 2017 on a season long loan during which he won the club's player of the year award. He made 39 appearances in all competitions scoring 14 times before returning to Chelsea.

Mount joined Championship club Derby County, managed by Lampard, on a season-long loan in July 2018, scoring a hat-trick in a 4-0 win against Bolton Wanderers and keeping Derby in contention for the promotion playoff.

In July 2019 he signed a new five-year contract with Chelsea and made his competitive debut in a 0-4 away defeat to Manchester United in the Premier League. He scored his first League goal a week later in a 1-1 draw against Leicester City, Lampard's home debut as manager at Stamford Bridge.

By July 2020 he became the first Chelsea Academy graduate to make his debut and complete 50 appearances in the same season.

Mount started the 2020-21 season well, featuring in all Chelsea's games. In January 2021 he captained Chelsea for the first time in a 3-1 win at home over Luton Town in the FA Cup. In March he scored the only goal in a 1-0 away victory over Liverpool, handing the hosts their fifth consecutive League defeat at Anfield for the first time in their history.

He made his senior England debut in September 2019 as a substitute against Bulgaria in UEFA Euro 2020 qualifying. He scored his first goal for England in November during a 4-0 away win against Kosovo in the same competition.

Mount's moment of magic at Stamford Bridge and Chelsea's journey to the Champions League Final in Porto started back in October 2020 in the group stages. The Blues kicked off with a goalless draw against Sevilla at The Bridge followed by an impressive 4-0 away win at the Krasnodar Stadium in Russia. They followed this with a 3-0 home victory against Rennes and a 2-1 away win in at the Roazhon Park stadium in France.

Chelsea's strong form continued in the return tie againt Sevilla at the Ramon Sanchez stadium in Spain with a 4-0 away win and qualifying was completed with a 1-1 draw with Krasnodar at Stamford Bridge.

The undefeated performances in the group stages set up a challenging round-of-16 tie against Spanish giants Atletico Madrid where Olivier Giroud scored a sublime overhead kick to give the Blues a 1-0 victory.

In a predictably tight encounter it was a piece of individul skill that proved to be the difference between the sides. Midway through the tense second half, the ball looped up in Giroud's direction. From 12 yards out and with his back to goal, he scissor-kicked the ball into the ground and beyond 'keeper Jan Oblak.

Initially disallowed for offside, VAR overturned the decision because the last touch had come off an Atleti defender. It was Atletico's second home European defeat in 30 games, the last one being by Chelsea in 2017!

In the second-leg goals from Moroccan Hakim Ziyech late in the first half and Emerson deep into added time at the end of the game completed a comprehensive win for the Blues.

Chelsea were back in Seville again for both the quarter-final ties against Porto as some Europen travel routes were restricted by Covid regulations.

Maiden European goals from Mount and Ben Chilwell helped Chelsea establish a crucial advantage over the Portuguese champions.

Mount's opener came just after the half-hour mark when he turned away from pressure and finished confidently into the bottom corner. Chilwell added a second with five minutes remaining by rounding the 'keeper and steering into an empty net.

Chelsea dominated the game in the return tie in Seville, however with seconds left Porto's Mehdi Taremi scored an overhead kick that gave Mendy no chance.

The 2-1 aggregate victory booked the Blues place in the semi-final clash against Real Madrid and the stage was set for Mount to give us some more magic.

GOAL 18
Deadly Zola fires blue army to victory

UEFA Cup Winners Cup Final. Chelsea 1-0 Stuttgart.
Wednesday, 13-05-1998 at the Rasunda Stadium, Stockholm, Sweden.
Attendance, 30,216. Gianfranco Zola (71 mins)

Team: Ed de Goey, Steve Clarke, Frank Leboeuf, Michael Duberry, Danny Granville, Dan Petrescu, Dennis Wise, Gustavo Poyet (Eddie Newton 81), Roberto Di Matteo, Gianluca Vialli, Tore Andre Flo (Gianfranco Zola 71).

IT was 7am on a dull morning at Gatwick but I managed a couple of pints of Guinness to settle the nerves before another European adventure.

I had worked until after midnight as one of the late team on a national newspaper. A quick nap, a shower and the Gatwick Express later I was waiting for my plane to Stockholm. But where was my brother?

Eventually, he trundled up just 90 minutes late. 'Must get some breakfast in mate, I'm starving. Where's McDonald's?'

So, as the last call for our flight was being made, I was watching a half-pounder and large fries rapidly disappearing. I heard a tale about a dodgy alarm clock, rail works, Tube delays and finally why it was too late to change pounds into Krona.' Then we sprinted for the gate. The last Chelsea fans on board.

As we made our walk of shame to the second row of seats from the rear of the plane the captain kindly explained that we had lost our take-off slot due to the late arrival of two passengers. Many of our fellow supporters then welcomed us with lively greetings.

Chelsea were about to play Stuttgart in the UEFA Cup Winners Cup Final in Stockholm at the Rasunda Stadium. The Swedish National arena was a controversial choice because of its limited capacity but Chelsea fans eventually numbered at least 20,000 of the 30,216 crowd.

Two years earlier the appointment of Ruud Gullit had sparked the trend of big name players from overseas heading for the Premiership. Chelsea bought Italians Gianluca Vialli and Roberto Di Matteo along with Frenchman Frank Leboeuf in the summer.

However, perhaps the clearest example of Gullit's desire to play 'sexy football' was the purchase of Italian international Gianfranco Zola from Parma for £4.5 million in November, 1996.

The Blues' route to the final began with a 2-0 victory over Slovan Bratislava at Stamford Bridge with goals from Danny Granville and Di Matteo, the job was finished by a 0-2 win in Slovakia with another goal from Di Matteo and a strike from Vialli.

In the second round Chelsea were drawn against Tromso IL, a club based in northern Norway, 217 miles north of the Arctic Circle. A 3-1 defeat in front of 6,438 spectators was blighted by snow and freezing conditions. A Vialli goal proved to be the only bright spot for the 300 Chelsea fans who made the arduous journey.

A 7-1 win at The Bridge with three goals for Vialli, two for Dan Petrescu and one each from Lebouf and Zola sealed the tie.

Real Betis proved slightly tougher opponents in the quarter-final, first-leg game at Benito Villamarin, Seville, however two goals from Tore Andre Flo gave Chelsea a deserved 1-2 victory. A second-leg 3-1 win with strikes from Frank Sinclair, Di Matteo and Zola put Chelsea in the semi-finals.

The first-leg tie against Vicenza Calico came just four days after Chelsea's victory over Middlesbrough in the League Cup Final in extra time at Wembley.

Over 1,250 made the trip to the Romeo Menti in Vicenza despite an all-day alcohol ban, but were disappointed to see their tired team go down to the only goal of the game.

There was an electric atmosphere for the return leg at Stamford Bridge but once again Vicenza scored early and were 2-0 up in the tie.

Chelsea now needed to score three goals. As Pasquale Lusio, the scorer, celebrated he put his finger to his lips suggesting Chelsea fans should be quiet.

However, the gesture achieved the opposite effect. Chelsea heads didn't go down and a crowd of 33,810 roared the Blues on to an equaliser three minutes later from Gustavo Poyet.

Soon after the break Vialli raced down the right to put in a cross from the edge of the Vicenza penalty area for Zola the smallest man on the pitch to score a powerful header past Pierluigi Brivio. Chelsea had 40 minutes to score one more goal. The tension and noise at The Bridge was almost unbearable.

Cometh the hour cometh the man. Mark Hughes replaced Jody Morris with 20 minutes to play. Five minutes later Hughes received a long clearance from Ed De Goey. The Welsh striker controlled the ball with a header, turned and lashed the ball into the net from the edge of the penalty area. Cue total pandemonium. The stadium erupted with passion, energy and joy. The Italians were down... and out.

Chelsea finished the League season in fourth place and as current holders of the League and FA Cups. However, there was one more match to play and it was the club's biggest game in Europe for nearly thirty years.

Vialli had some major selection decisions to make. Zola was only partially fit following a groin strain and Mark Hughes had started in every game since the semi-final. In the end he picked himself over Hughes and Flo over Zola.

Chelsea controlled the early stages but Stuttgart played their way back into the game. De Goey made a fine save from a Krassmir Balakov shot and Dennis Wise volleyed just wide.

In the 71st minute Vialli made his move - he decided to bring on Zola for Flo. Following a throw-in Chelsea possession led to the ball being laid off to Wise who found Zola, but the Italian was quickly challenged. The ball came back to Wise who saw Zola had continued his run and found him with an exquisite through ball which was dispatched by the maestro.

Zola had scored just 18 seconds after coming on. Chelsea fans in all four stands of the stadium went berserk and Zola celebrated with the fans packed behind the goal. There was still time for Romanian Dan Petrescu to be given a straight red card for a challenge on Murat Yakin. Then the Blues had done it, the cup kings became the first English Club to win the cup Winners Cup twice.

After the match Zola said, 'It was quite incredible for me. I couldn't contain myself. It was one of the best moments of my career.

'I want to thank the masseur who treated me for a groin injury. Mimmo Pezza did a fantastic job. You must imagine my situation. Eighteen days ago, my dream turned into nothing. Then after treatment, suddenly I'm in the match. I came in, scored and we won the cup.'

When Ruud Gullit signed Zola in 1996 he said, 'I think with Gianfranco that his qualities are obvious. He has great technical ability and he sees the game very well. I think it's vital for us that he is the sort of player who can decide a game with his vision, technique and ability to open it up from even ordinary situations.'

And Sir Alex Ferguson after watching Zola score against Manchester United in February 1997 said, 'He's a clever little so-and-so, much better than I thought.'

Sir Alex again, post retirement said, 'Little Gianfranco Zola, he annoyed me. He was one of these players who was unperturbed about who he was playing against. He always seemed to have a smile on his face.

'How can he be enjoying himself playing against United? Nobody else does. He was a fantastic player and I loved watching him.'

Former chairman Ken Bates said, 'Zola was undoubtedly one of Chelsea's greatest players ever. He's been a joy to watch and a great influence both on and off the field.'

In August 1999 Zola's chip set Gus Poyet up for one of the most memorable Chelsea goals ever in a 4-0 win over Sunderland. Poyet said, 'The best I've ever played with, no doubt. I used to marvel at him in training each day. Gianfranco made you a better player, he knew what I was going to do before I'd even thought of it.'

And Zola himself on his unforgettable backheel volley against Norwich City in the FA Cup in January 2002 said, 'Don't ask me how I did it, because I don't know. It is one of those goals you could try 100 times and it will probably never come off again.'

Former Chelsea manager Claudio Ranieri said the goal was a moment of brilliance, 'Fantasy, magic. Only Maradona or Pele, only the big players, would do something like that. Gianfranco tries everything because he is a wizard and the wizard must try.'

Zola's goal against Stuttgart confirmed what every Chelsea fan knows, the little Italian is unique. He said, 'I think my way around the pitch, always changing my pattern to make it difficult for opponents. I can twist away quickly and stay on my feet. I'm also strong for my size.'

After the game my brother and I, along with 16,000 other exuberant Chelsea fans, joined the long, long convoy of coaches to the airport. After about 90 minutes of gridlock most supporters alighted and walked to the terminal where more chaos was in progress.

Normal procedures seemed to have broken down and fans were being put on any plane to Gatwick. I had a chance for one seat on a flight but needed another one for my brother, now sound asleep. The seat was gladly snapped up by comedian David Baddiel.

After about four hours we finally found a couple of spare seats and jetted away from a famous victory. Back in London a new day had dawned, the Tube was running and we headed back to West London for some sleep, after a few pints in Ealing. You have to really. Cheers Zola and Come on you Blues.

Before leaving for Cagliari in 2003 Zola summed up his feelings, 'Chelsea is the place where I received everything I was dreaming of when I first started playing football. The fans gave me everything I was looking for. They made me feel a very, very important player, even when I wasn't playing very well. I felt special since day one here.'

GOAL 17
Bridge sparks power shift in capital

UEFA CL Quarter-final second-leg. Arsenal 1-2 Chelsea
(First-leg 1-1, Chelsea win 3-2 on aggregate)
Tuesday, 06-04-2004 at Highbury.
Attendance, 35,486. Wayne Bridge (87)

Team: Marco Ambrosio, Mario Melchiot, John Terry, William Gallas, Wayne Bridge, Scott Parker (Jesper Gronkjaer 46), Frank Lampard, Claude Makelele, Damien Duff (Joe Cole 82), Eidur Gudjohnsen, Jimmy Floyd Hasselbaink (Crespo 82).

STRANDED for work in a dark and rainswept corner of Lancashire, I managed to find a village pub with a television showing Chelsea's Champion's League game.

Despite the fixture being a London Derby, a dozen or so flat-capped farmers around the bar soon made it clear they were keen to see Chelsea completely demolished.

However, despite those doomsayers, all these years later Wayne Bridge still has Chelsea fans telling him how his Champions League winner sparked a changing of the guard in London.

The former England left-back only managed ten goals in his 16-year professional career. By far the most significant was his beautiful 87th minute strike at Highbury that won the quarter-final against Arsene Wenger's Gunners in April 2004.

Arsenal, who had drawn 1-1 at Stamford Bridge in the first-leg, were the best side in England at the time, they lifted the Premier League that season and still had Thierry Henry and Patrick Vieira.

Chelsea were in their first campaign in the Roman Abramovich era and were full of new signings, including Bridge, who joined from Southampton for £7 million plus Graeme Le Saux.

Bridge said, 'Everyone talks about the changing of the guard. It definitely went that way.

'Everyone would have said Chelsea always struggled against Arsenal but things definitely swayed after that.

'It was the early years of Chelsea spending money and bringing players in.'

Bridge can still remember the celebrations in the dressing room after the match, 'I remember Roman coming in afterwards and he was buzzing. The whole dressing room was dancing around asking for extra bonuses.

'He can be quiet and sometimes I think it's the language thing, but he definitely understands. He's a very intelligent guy who has done wonders for Chelsea.'

In an absolutely enthralling match Jose Antonio Reyes fired Arsenal into the lead in first-half injury time. But Frank Lampard drew the Blues level after a Lehmann mistake before Bridge sealed a famous win.

Arsenal, with Henry and Reyes back in the starting line-up, were pegged back by waves of Chelsea pressure in the opening minutes. But Lampard had the only real sight of goal, firing straight at 'keeper Jens Lehmann.

In a full-blooded performance Chelsea's William Gallas and Jimmy Floyd Hasselbaink were both shown yellow cards, while between the bookings Henry hit a fierce right-foot shot over the bar.

He had an even better chance after 18 minutes from a clever through pass from Reyes, but his shot drifted wide.

A classy move by Damien Duff on 20 minutes nearly put Chelsea ahead, breaking clear he cut inside Sol Campbell before sending the ball inches wide.

The action continued with chances at both ends but just as Chelsea looked to go in at half-time all square, Reyes scored from close range with the last kick of the half.

Jesper Gronkjaer replaced Scott Parker at half-time as manager Claudio Ranieri looked to boost Chelsea's attacking options. The change worked as Chelsea celebrated an equaliser within just six minutes of the restart.

Lampard was in the right place to pounce after Claude Makelele's long-range strike was spilled by Lehmann. But the England international was holding his head moments later after a wonderful 25-yard strike curled into the side netting with Lehmann beaten.

It was no more than Chelsea deserved for their battling response to Reyes' goal, but with scores level, both sides became more cautious.

However, Reyes still looked lively and his left-foot shot was pushed away by Ambrosio. Shortly afterwards the Italian 'keeper had to be alert to tip away Toure's 40-yard effort.

With 10 minutes left, Dennis Bergkamp came on for Henry for Arsenal, while Chelsea brought on Joe Cole and Hernan Crespo for Duff and Hasselbaink.

Chelsea pressed again, and Ashley Cole made a goal-line clearance from Eidur Gudjohnsen as the home side's defence disintegrated on 85 minutes.

But England defender Bridge popped up two minutes later to rifle home a left-foot finish after being set up by a perfect one-two with Gudjohnsen to end Arsenal's unbeaten run against the Blues and send the Chelsea fans ballistic.

After the game Chelsea manager Claudio Ranieri said, 'I am mad with joy at the result.'

Bridge was born in Southampton in August, 1980, but moved to the parish of Oliver's Battery, Winchester at an early age.

He attended Oliver's Battery Primary and Kings' School, Winchester. When playing for Oliver's Battery in around 1994, he was spotted by former Saints player Micky Adams who recommended him to Southampton, who then signed him as a trainee in July 1996.

He was a graduate of the Southampton Academy where he made his debut in 1998. He also played for Chelsea, West Ham, Manchester City,

Fulham and Sunderland during his Premier League career and was capped 36 times for England.

Bridge was fast, determined, skilful and full of youthful promise and his forward runs became an exciting sight at The Dell and then at St Mary's. He was an ever-present as Saints finished their first season at their new stadium comfortably in mid-table.

Bridge's temperament and consistency, together with a high level of fitness, enabled him to continue to play every match until January 2003 when he limped off with an injury in a defeat to Liverpool.

This brought to an end a run of 113 consecutive appearances, a Premier League record for an outfield player, since beaten by Lampard with 164.

After five years with the Saints bigger clubs were trailing Bridge and he was finally tempted away to join Chelsea in the 2003 close season.

He was initially a regular starter and his finest moment was the goal described here against Arsenal, but he also scored against Besiktas and Portsmouth in the 2003-04 season.

Bridge started the 2004-05 season playing regularly under new manager Jose Mourinho but he picked up a serious ankle injury in an FA Cup tie against Newcastle United which ended his season. Chelsea went on to win the Premier League in his absence but Bridge had already made enough appearances to collect a winners' medal.

In the 2005-06 season Chelsea had signed Spanish left-back Asier del Horno and Bridge struggled to regain his place in the team. He only made two appearances for Chelsea that season, both in domestic cup games. The Blues won the Premier League again, but Bridge was not eligible for a medal.

Bridge's main competition for a place in the side for the 2006-07 campaign came from fellow England international left-back Ashley Cole. He played the full game in Chelsea's 3-0 victory over Manchester City on the opening day, supplying a cross for the third goal, a header from Didier Drogba.

However, Bridge's strong early season form wasn't enough to hold down the left-back position with Mourinho preferring Ashley Cole in most games.

Following Cole's injury in the 3-0 Premier League victory over Blackburn Rovers early in 2007, Bridge became Chelsea's natural choice for left-back.

Bridge featured in attack for the injury hit Blues at League Two side Wycombe Wanderers in the League Cup semi-final first-leg match, scoring in the 1-1 draw.

He finished the season with two cup final winner's medals after playing in the League Cup Final against Arsenal in a 2-1 win and the 1-0 victory over Manchester United in the FA Cup Final.

Bridge's Chelsea career ended in January 2009 when Manchester City agreed an undisclosed fee for the left-back, thought to be in the region of £10 million.

Speaking soon after Lampards's appointment as Chelsea manager he looked back on his time with the Blues with pride and believed Lampard can build a strong career in management.

Lampard and Bridge spent six seasons together at Stamford Bridge and the retired defender was confident Lamps has the potential to guide a crop of youngsters and some new recruits to success.

Bridge highlighted Lampard's work ethic and said, 'If he gets the chance to buy the right players and is given time I can't see why they couldn't build a title winning side.'

'With the way they play and the young players getting a chance, they are going in the right direction.

'If it's confidence they need then I'm sure Lamps will give it to them. They could not have a better person than Frank, with all his experience, to learn from. It's great for the young kids. I hope they keep playing well and can go on to achieve some success.'

Looking back through the years to his own glory days and his iconic goal against Arsenal for the Blues, Bridge said: 'Whenever I have the opportunity to chat to fans they always talk about how from that moment things changed. The balance of power had swung irrevocably in our favour and Chelsea were always a better team after that night.'

In darkest Lancashire it was still pouring with rain and the flat-capped farmers around the bar were not happy. They weren't happy with the result, they moaned about the wild celebrations of the Chelsea fans and they clearly disagreed about the Blues' potential. However, your author simply finished his pint, made his excuses and left the building.

GOAL 16
Di Matteo magic after just 43 seconds

FA Cup Final. Chelsea 2-0 Middlesbrough.

Saturday, 27-05-1997 at Wembley.

Attendance, 79,160. Roberto Di Matteo (43 secs)

Team: Frode Grodas, Dan Petrescu, Steve Clarke, Frank Leboeuf, Frank Sinclair, Scott Minto, Dennis Wise, Roberto Di Matteo, Eddie Newton, Mark Hughes, Gianfranco Zola (Gianluca Vialli 89).

AS Roberto Di Matteo wheeled away to celebrate his opening goal just 43 seconds into the FA Cup Final he tried to find a face in the crowd. Up in the stands was his sister Concetta, who is blind, and was being told the mayhem going on around her had been caused by her brother's early strike.

'It's going to remain always on my mind. I think it's destiny,' said Di Matteo. 'I couldn't even think about something like that.'

Cup finals are usually cagey encounters until early nerves settle and the managers' game plans start to take hold. However, Di Matteo was having none of that. He picked up the ball in his own half, some 70-yards out from the Middlesbrough goal.

He said, 'I had space in front of me and started to run. Ah well, let me just try something because the game has just started.

'One defender went with Sparky (Mark Hughes) and the other came up a little but was quite far, so maybe didn't expect me to shoot.'

From more than 30-yards he did and the ball flew through 'keeper Ben Robert's arms, grazed the underside of the bar and nestled into the net.

'I felt it straight away and when I saw the ball it was incredible,' said

Di Matteo. 'I hit the ball at the front of my foot. Usually you shoot with your whole foot, but because it came from the front of my foot it went up and then down over the goalkeeper. It had to happen. It was my day.'

It was Ruud Gullit's day as well because Middlesbrough never looked like threatening his achievement of becoming the first foreigner to manage an FA Cup winning team.

The game was almost over as soon as it started with Di Matteo's knockout blow. Chelsea won the FA Cup for the second time and were so superior on the day that Middlesbrough never really recovered from the setback. Eddie Newton finally made it 2-0 in the 83rd minute with another excellent goal.

Gullit's counterpart, Bryan Robson, was left to pick up the pieces after the Teeside club lost two Wembley finals and were relegated to the First Division.

Chelsea made a sensational start to the match on a steamy, humid afternoon. Di Matteo picked up a pass from skipper Dennis Wise, who had won the ball from Robbie Mustoe, the Italy midfielder ran unchallenged from inside his own half before dipping the ball over the young Middlesbrough 'keeper.

It was a blow made possible not only by Di Matteo's mastery of technique but by a clever run by Mark Hughes that removed Mark Pearson as the last line of defence.

Juninho briefly raised Middlesbrough's hopes with a through ball, but Frode Grodas beat Phil Stamp to it with a well-timed dash from goal.

Fabrizio Ravanelli limped off the field after 21 minutes after an unsuccessful attempt to beat Frank Sinclair to a through ball. Only five minutes after Mikkel Beck had replaced Ravanelli, Middlesbrough made another substitution, Steve Vickers replacing Mustoe.

Chelsea's midfield domination gave them more scoring chances in the first half. Pearson headed a Dan Petrescu lob off the goal-line, while Roberts had to fling himself across his line to stop a Zola free-kick.

Middlesbrough's Gianluca Festa was frustrated in stoppage time at the end of the first 45 minutes when his far post header was correctly disallowed for offside. After 64 minutes Frank Leboeuf failed to cut out Beck's back-header from Clayton Blackmore's long throw but Pearson prodded the ball wide.

For a long-time Chelsea seemed unwilling to go in search of a second but nevertheless Middlesbrough were unable to pierce the resilient Blues' defence.

In one cameo Gianfranco Zola beat three men before cutting back from the byline for a shot which Roberts saved at his near post.

Juninho had little impact on the match until the last 20 minutes when he began what appeared to be a running feud with Leboeuf. Fouled by the French defender he used the free kick to release Vickers for a shot Grodas saved with his legs.

However, Middlesbrough's final attempt to draw level cost them dear as Chelsea hit them on the break. The ball shuttled between Newton and Petrescu before the Romanian chipped a pass to Zola, running in at the far post. It looked to be going behind him, but the Italian brilliantly flicked the ball back with the outside of his right foot.

Midfielder Newton, following up in the middle of the goalmouth, simply had to steer the ball into the net with his left foot as it bounced in front of him. The stadium erupted as the blue and white hordes celebrated the 83rd minute strike that made it 2-0.

It was the signal for Gullit to let Vialli have his two minutes of fame as substitute for Zola and for the stadium to fill with the sound of Blue Is The Colour celebrating Chelsea's victory in the 116th FA Cup Final.

Chelsea's 43 second goal hero Di Matteo was born in Schaffhausen, Switzerland to Italian parents from Abruzzo. He began his career with Swiss club Schaffhausen, before joining Aarau in 1991. He won the Swiss Nationalliga A with Aarau in 1993.

He signed for Lazio in the summer of 1993 on a free transfer. Di Matteo became a regular member of the Lazio side in midfield under managers Dino Zoff and later Zdenek Zeman, and he made his debut for the Italian national team during his three seasons with the Rome club.

Di Matteo scored the winner against Middlesbrough on his home debut for Chelsea in the summer of 1996. He contributed nine goals in his first season, including long-range efforts against both Tottenham Hotspur and Wimbledon.

He helped the club finish sixth place in the League, their highest placing since 1989-90, and reach the 1997 FA Cup Final. Di Matteo's goal was the fastest in a Wembley FA Cup final until the record was broken by Louis Saha for Everton in their 2-1 defeat by Chelsea in 2009.

The following season Di Matteo again proved his worth to the team, contributing ten goals and numerous assists, as Chelsea went on to claim the League Cup and the Cup Winners' Cup, their first European honour since 1971.

In the League Cup Final, again against Middlesbrough, Di Matteo scored the second goal in a 2–0 win. Di Matteo played in midfield next to Gustavo Poyet, Wise, and Petrescu in the 1998-1999 season as Chelsea finished third.

During the 1999-2000 season Di Matteo was side-lined by injury but returned late in the campaign to score a handful of crucial goals, including his third Cup-winning goal at Wembley.

In a poor FA Cup Final, Di Matteo capitalised on a mistake by Aston Villa goalkeeper David James to score the winner in the 72nd minute, handing Chelsea their fourth major trophy in three years.

This victory led Di Matteo to comment on the old Wembley Stadium, 'It's a shame they're tearing the old place down, it has been a very lucky ground for me.'

Early into the 2000-2001 season, Di Matteo sustained a triple leg fracture in a UEFA Cup tie against Swiss side St. Gallen and did not play for the next eighteen months.

He gave up on hopes of returning from this injury in February 2002 and retired from playing at the age of 31. In his six years on the pitch at Chelsea, Di Matteo made 175 appearances and scored 26 goals.

Di Matteo's managerial career has included spells at Milton Keynes Dons, West Bromwich Albion and in 2011-12 he was appointed assistant to Andre Villas Boas at Chelsea. In March 2012 following the dismissal of

Boas he became caretaker manager of Chelsea until the end of the season. He brought in Newton, former Chelsea teammate and scorer of the second goal in the 1997 Cup Final, to work as his assistant.

On May 19, 2012, he guided Chelsea to victory in the UEFA Champions League Final, defeating Bayern Munich at their own Allianz Arena. The match ended 1-1 after extra time with Chelsea coming out victorious in the penalty shootout.

Looking back on Di Matteo's 1997 Wembley goal teammate Sinclair said, 'I was bombing down the right expecting him to pass. I was thinking 'What's he doing?' Suddenly, it's in the back of the net. It was mind blowing.

'We were hyped up. We were trounced by Manchester United in 1994. I was 22-years-old and excited about Wembley, but nobody mentioned how bad it was if you were beaten.

'We lost 4-0, I gave away a penalty and I was devastated. It left a bad taste and I knew the only way to get rid of it was to go back in 1997 and win.'

Di Matteo simply said, 'In the FA Cup you always have to expect the unexpected.'

GOAL 15
Poyet scissors-kick cuts the mustard

Premier League. Chelsea 4-0 Sunderland.
Saturday, 07-08-1999 at Stamford Bridge.
Attendance 34,831 (Gus Poyet 20, 78).

Team, Ed de Goey, Albert Ferrer, Marcel Desailly, Frank Leboeuf, Graeme Le Saux, Dan Petrescu (Roberto Di Matteo 86), Dennis Wise, Didier Deschamps, Gustavo Poyet (Celestine Babayaro 79), Chris Sutton (Tore Andre Flo 73), Gianfranco Zola.

THE man from Montevideo scored a wonderful scissors-kick goal to complete a classy opening day display from Chelsea.

In a game dominated almost entirely by the Blues, the home side could have made it even more thanks to a flurry of great of chances.

Man of the match was midfielder Poyet, whose double strike was completed by a memorable volley to seal victory in a totally one-sided encounter.

However, he was ably supported by Sunderland's chief tormentor, fellow goal-scorer Gianfranco Zola, and new signing Didier Deschamps, while substitute Tore Andre Flo hit Chelsea's other goal.

It has been many years, but Poyet still has vivid memories of the strike that remains one of the best-ever in Chelsea's history.

The Uruguayan said, 'I wasn't a player who tried that strike before, or even after.

'It wasn't something you would do naturally every day, it just happened that day without explanation.

'When Gianfranco controlled the ball with an incredible touch, I was running from outside the box and it's a moment that I am expecting him to pass the ball to me,' Poyet added. 'The understanding you get with the special players, he kind of waited for me. It was like, 'Go on, keep running, don't worry – the ball will drop in front of you somehow'.

'He was waiting for me to run, so I kept running. He was looking at me and I kept running, and the ball dropped perfectly in front of me to do that action.'

Poyet is aware that wonderful goals like that don't come along very often, but praises Zola for his exceptional assist.

'Sometimes, when you're running into the box as a midfielder and you go past the ball, you learn how to turn and do an overhead kick.

'That's an action that you practise, one that happens in training and in games. Most of the time you won't score but you've got that action in your head because of how many times you've done it.

'This kind of action, I don't even know what to call it, scissors or whatever – I didn't practise it.

'I didn't do it before or even try it before, so I can't explain why it happened that day. I suppose it was natural.

'The kick was very clean but the pass was exceptional. If you try it a hundred times, that would probably be the best you can get it.'

He adds, 'Every year my son or someone else in Uruguay sends me the video because it's on Twitter or somewhere.

'I'm not on social media, so I don't see it until someone sends it to me. Then I see it again. It's always coming back to me.'

Poyet gave Chelsea the lead against Sunderland after 20 minutes with an unmarked header from Dennis Wise's left-wing corner-kick, a text-book example of the late run from midfield. As Thomas Sorensen, Sunderland's Danish goalkeeper rushed out, Poyet held his nerve to meet the dipping ball.

Zola then skipped past Steve Bould to fire home a second and allow the Chelsea faithful to relax in the sunshine.

Just as Sunderland were attempting to claw their way back into the match, they were punished by the Blues in a vintage three-minute spell of attacking flair and ruthless finishing from the Stamford Bridge hitmen.

First Dan Petrescu played a one-two with Zola before crossing for the unmarked Flo to head home just a few minutes after coming on as substitute.

Then Poyet scored the goal of the game as he capitalised on Zola's vision by thundering home a first-time scissors-kick after the Italian had chipped the ball into his path.

That move had been set up by a perceptive long pass to Zola from Didier Deschamps, whose Chelsea debut was convincing enough to mean France's captain may play an important part in Gianluca Vialli's expensive jigsaw.

Patrolling the space in front of his international colLeagues, Marcel Desailly and Frank Leboeuf, in the first half Deschamps performed his customary duties of interception and distribution with unfussy expertise.

There was still enough time for Flo to head just wide and for Sorensen to make an inspired diving save to deny another substitute, Roberto Di Matteo, before Sunderland's misery was ended by the referee's final whistle.

Afterwards Vialli was all diplomacy when asked about two openings crafted by Deschamps and Zola respectively for Chis Sutton, Chelsea's £10 million signing from Blackburn.

'I always had problems when I started with a new club,' the Chelsea manager said. 'It's too easy otherwise. You go, you score, you become a hero straight away. It's better to work your socks off.'

And he added, he judged his strikers by criteria other than the number of goals they score.

'If you go on to the pitch just thinking about scoring goals, you forget about the other important things,' he said.

Poyet was born in Montevideo, the capital and largest city in Uruguay in November 1967. The city is situated on the southern coast of the country, on the north-eastern bank of the Rio de la Plata.

The city was established in 1724 by a Spanish soldier, Bruno Mauricio de Zabal, as a strategic move amidst the Spanish-Portuguese dispute over the region. Montevideo hosted every match during the first

FIFA World Cup in 1930. Described as a 'vibrant, eclectic place with a rich cultural life' and 'a thriving tech centre with an entrepreneurial culture.'

It is the hub of commerce and higher education in Uruguay as well as its chief port. The city is also the financial hub of Uruguay and the cultural anchor of a metropolitan area with a population of around 2 million.

Poyet, a goal-scoring midfielder, began his career with spells at Grenoble and River Plate. He moved to Real Zaragoza in Spain in 1990, winning the Copa del Rey in 1994 and the Cup Winners' Cup a year later beating Arsenal in the final.

He became Zaragoza's longest-serving foreign player and scored 60 goals in 240 games for the club.

Poyet joined Chelsea on a free transfer in June 1997, but not long into his first season he suffered cruciate ligament damage.

The injury meant he missed the team's 2-0 victory over Middlesbrough in the 1998 League Cup Final, but recovered in time for the 1-0 win over VfB Stuttgart in the European Cup Winners' Cup Final.

The following season he contributed 14 goals, making him the club's second highest scorer, to help Chelsea finish third in the Premiership including a crucial headed goal in the 1-0 win against Leeds United.

The South American also scored the winner for Chelsea in the 1998 UEFA Super Cup 1-0 victory over Real Madrid at the Stade Louis II in Monaco.

In 1999-2000 he scored 18 goals, which again made him Chelsea's second highest scorer, including the scissor-kick volley against Sunderland.

Poyet also scored a long-range strike against Lazio and both Chelsea's goals in the FA Cup semi-final against Newcastle United among the most memorable, as the team won the FA Cup Final 1-0 against Aston Villa and reached the UEFA Champions League quarter-finals.

With the arrival of new manager Claudio Ranieri in September 2000,

Chelsea moved into a time of transition. With Ranieri aiming to build a younger squad, Poyet requested a transfer.

The midfielder made 145 appearances for Chelsea and scored 49 goals. He moved to Tottenham Hotspur for around £2.2 million in May 2001.

After his playing career ended Poyet moved into management. He served under Wise as assistant manager at Swindon Town and Leeds United, and Juande Ramos at Tottenham.

In November 2009 Poyet was appointed manager of Brighton & Hove Albion and in his first full season as manager led the club to promotion as League One Champions, for which he was named League One Manager of the Year.

In October 2013 he was hired by Premier League Sunderland and guided them to the League Cup Final in his first season but was sacked in March 2015 after a run of poor results.

He has since had spells at clubs abroad including Greek side AEK Athens, La Liga side Real Betis, Chinese team Shanghai Shenhua and French side Bordeaux.

When Poyet left Chelsea in May 2001 the club was just beginning its transformation into consistent winners under Roman Abramovich.

Poyet said about his time with the Blues, 'At Chelsea we were beautiful but champions have to win ugly.'

And reflecting on his career he said, 'When I was with Chelsea we spoke about football the whole time, but it was different at Tottenham. Some of the players had things too easy. They had the best cars by the age of 21, whereas when I played we had to wait until we were 30.'

GOAL 14
Rhoades-Brown humbles Euro Reds

FAC Fifth Round. Chelsea 2 - 0 Liverpool.

Saturday, 13-02-82 at Stamford Bridge.

Attendance, 41,422. Peter Rhoades-Brown (8)

Team: Steve Francis, Gary Locke, Chris Hutchings, Micky Nutton, Micky Droy, Colin Pates, Peter Rhoades-Brown, Kevin Hales, Colin Lee, Clive Walker, Mike Fillery.

CHELSEA of the Second Division had struggled through to the glamour tie of the FA Cup 5th round against Liverpool the reigning European Champions.

Goalless draws at Stamford Bridge against Hull and Wrexham had been followed by 0-2 and 1-1 away performances to progress.

It wasn't until training the day before the game that manager John Neal finalised his team and young Peter Rhoades-Brown, 20, knew he was in the starting-eleven.

Rhoades-Brown had been on Chelsea's books since he was 12-years-old and was still living in Hampton, Richmond upon Thames, with his mother Joan and father Roy.

The excitement for the family was tempered by the fact that Roy - a lifelong Liverpool supporter - was in hospital in Maida Vale, London for treatment for hydrocephalus, a build-up of fluid on his brain.

Despite these concerns Rhoades-Brown knew his dad would want him to enjoy the day. He kept to his routine of lots of pasta for dinner and an early night on the Friday before the game. In the morning he was up by 8am and as usual on matchday ate a bowl of Frosties followed by three Weetabix with lots of sugar to boost his energy.

'I had a routine for home matches,' said Rhoades-Brown, 'Breakfast, then I would wash my car, a white Volkswagen Beetle. Norman Medhurst our physio called it *me time*.

'We had done our homework on their players, big names like Terry McDermott, Alan Hansen, Mark Lawrenson and Kenny Dalglish. They were all household names. I concentrated on the skills and possible weaknesses of Phil Neal who was likely to be marking me.'

Rhoades-Brown's father, Roy, had told him, 'My ideal would be that you score and have a great game, but Liverpool win 1-2.' With this in mind Rhoades-Brown, or Rosie as he was known to his teammates, wrote a brief letter to the opposing manager, the legendary Bob Paisley.

He wrote, 'Dear Mr Paisley, this is Peter Rhoades-Brown from Chelsea FC. As you know we will be playing you in the FA Cup at Stamford Bridge soon. My dad who is a dedicated Liverpool supporter will be undergoing surgery days before the game. I wondered if it would be possible to organize a card signed by all the lads to wish him well?'

With all the commitments before the biggest game of the round Rhoades-Brown thought there was no chance his request would be granted. However, 20 minutes before kick-off Medhurst answered a knock on the dressing room door.

There's someone to see you he told Rhoades-Brown. Paisley stood at the door with a bag containing a red No. 4 shirt signed by all his players.

'Have a good game, son,' said Paisley.

Rhoades-Brown hadn't told his teammates about the letter, knowing the stick he would receive. However, Medhurst was in on the secret and used the gift to great psychological effect, 'Rosie, I had a dream last night that they would give you a shirt. It's a sign. It's going to be your day!'

The players had gathered at Hotel Lily in Lillie Road, near the ground at 11am for their pre-match meal of chicken, beans and toast. Captain Micky Droy and Colin Pates made a point of looking after all the younger players and trying to dispel any nerves.

Striker Clive Walker had been in the team four years previously when Chelsea achieved the shock of the third round by beating Liverpool 4-2 at The Bridge. He told the group, 'We've done it before and we can do it again. Come on!'

Rhoades-Brown and his teammates drove their own cars to the ground and parked behind the East Stand. In the changing room quietly spoken boss Neal re-emphasized the need to play a quick, pressing game, keeping possession and moving up and down the pitch as a unit.

Physio Medhurst buzzed from player to player offering words of encouragement. Rhoades-Brown felt nervous but calmed down a lot after the visit from Paisley. He had borrowed one of his dad's ties to wear with his matchday suit to make him feel closer to his father on the big day.

Chelsea were lying eighth in the Second Division while Liverpool were the reigning European champions and would go on to win the League title that season.

Early in the match winger Rhoades-Brown latched onto a loose ball in midfield and after a clear run at goal slid the ball past Bruce Grobbelaar for the opener in the eighth minute.

Rhoades-Brown said, 'Once I had slipped past McDermott I knew I was quick and no one was going to catch me. On the way through on goal I thought I've got to score. I'll be the hero or I'll be absolutely crucified.

'I didn't hit it particularly well, it skimmed off the surface but it was enough to beat Grobbelaar to his left.'

Walker and Colin Lee were among the first players to celebrate with him after the goal, he remembers one of them said we thought you would miss.

'The noise level when I scored was just incredible, it was unbelievable. The East Stand, the West Stand and the benches were all up on their feet roaring, waving scarves and flags. The over-flowing Shed was a sea of bodies and had gone completely ballistic.'

Rhoades-Brown had scored his first goal of the season not in a mid-table clash with 10,000 spectators but in front of 40,000 of the Chelsea faithful at Stamford Bridge.

'Later I was slated by the others for swinging my arm around as we jogged back to kick-off again. I think I was a bit numb, The Shed was in full voice singing, 'We shall not, we shall not be moved,' I get that tingling feeling again just talking about it.

'I thought of my mum and brother behind the dugout and my dad listening on the radio in hospital. I couldn't breathe properly for about ten minutes after the goal. I was desperately trying to suck in oxygen then, suddenly, I was back.

Rhoades-Brown knew there was a lot more work to do as Liverpool pressed and harried to create chances later in the game. Chelsea remained composed with Droy marshaling more men behind the ball and Pates completing a solid man-for-man marking job on Graeme Souness as the clock ticked down.

However, six minutes from full time, a Walker cross from the right caused a dreadful mix-up in the Liverpool defence with Grobbelaar bouncing into Alan Hansen, leaving Lee with a tap in to seal a famous upset.

Left-winger Rhoades-Brown said the noise from the East Stand was again immense. At 2-0 the pressure was off and in a maelstrom of emotions he briefly wondered whether the second goal would take the edge off his own strike.

After injury time the referee finally blew the whistle for full time. Sammy Lee was the first to shake Rhoades-Brown by the hand. 'You deserved that. Well done,' said the Liverpool and England midfielder.

Rhoades-Brown said, 'Thousands of jubilant Chelsea fans invaded the pitch so it took an age to get back to the dressing room. Back in the dressing room chairman Ken Bates came down to tell the players how proud he was of the team.

A case of beer was provided for the players to celebrate and manager Neal and assistant manager Ian McNeil, such a significant partnership for Chelsea in the early 1980s, congratulated the team on a great performance. Meanwhile, physio Medhurst reminded Rhoades-Brown that he had predicted the victory.

As some of his teammates left for the players' bar, Rhoades-Brown drove to the hospital in Maida Vale where his dad was a patient. Roy had listened to the commentary on the radio but was not the type of man to dish out too many compliments.

Rhoades-Brown drove home and spent the evening with his mum Joan and his brother. Joan was always the first spectator to take her seat at The Bridge when he was playing.

'She would sit behind the dugout with her flask of coffee for hours beforehand. She was absolutely brilliant, just a great mum,' said Rhoades Brown.

The next day Rhoades-Brown visited his dad again as highlights of the game were being shown on *The Big Match.*

'About five patients in dressing gowns and bandages were sitting on armchairs in the TV room watching the programme,' said Rhoades-Brown. 'It looked like a scene from *One Flew Over the Cuckoo's Nest.*'

Rhoades-Brown joined them for his goal and Roy said, 'Not a bad finish son. I think I taught you how to do that.'

And in Brian Moore's interview with Rhoades-Brown, his dad exclaimed, 'That's where my bloody tie's gone.'

'The game was definitely the highlight of my career,' said Rhoades-Brown. 'I joined Chelsea at 12-years of age so it was a boyhood dream come true. The goal was a magical moment I'll savour all my life.'

GOAL 13
Ivanovic and old guard topple Napoli

UEFA CL Round of 16 second-leg. Chelsea 4-1 Napoli.
(First-leg 1-3. Chelsea win 5-4 on agg)
Wednesday, 14-03-2012 at Stamford Bridge.
Attendance, 37,784. Branislav Ivanovic (104)

Team: Petr Cech, Branislav Ivanovic, David Luiz, John Terry (Jose
Bosingwa 97), Ashley Cole, Daniel Sturridge (Fernando Torres 62),
Michael Essien, Frank Lampard, Ramires, Juan Mata, Florent Malouda,
Didier Drogba.

THERE have been some historic nights at Stamford Bridge over the last
century but few could compare with the sheer intensity of this
performance.

Captain John Terry's old guard simply would not surrender. They
came roaring back from a first-leg 3-1 defeat inflicted at the Stadio San
Paulo by a classy Napoli side.

Terry, battling back only three weeks after surgery on a knee injury,
said this could be one of the great nights at The Bridge. He was proved
right. Ramires ran until you thought he could not possibly run any further.
Then he ran again.

At the end of extra time Michael Essien was playing at centre half
because David Luiz could no longer run. Peter Cech, Didier Drogba,
Frank Lampard and Branislav Ivanovic had all played vital roles and the
whole team were on their knees.

Temporary manager Roberto Di Matteo and the ecstatic Stamford
Bridge faithful must have thought they were living a dream as they
celebrated after this extraordinary performance

Three weeks earlier the Blues had been left with a tough job after conceding three goals in Italy.

Ezequiel Lavezzi had hit an unstoppable shot in the 37th minute and beat Cech again in the 64th minute while Cavani had swept home on the stroke of half-time. Chelsea had opened the scoring when Juan Mata pounced on a scuffed ball in Napoli's area to score from ten yards.

Ivanovic said, 'One of the small but good things to come out of that game was the away goal which gave us a chance to believe.'

Back at The Bridge the tension was mounting in anticipation of another great European comeback. The area around the stadium and the road from Fulham Broadway Underground station was packed hours before kick-off.

All the local hostelries were heaving by 5pm. Many Chelsea fans had finished early from work, some old faces had tuned up for this game. Proper Chels. There was a tangible feeling of excitement in the air.

This could be the last chance for some of the old guard. After all the disappointments of recent campaigns could this be the year for European glory? Terry was back in the team, the Italians wouldn't like a cold night in London, the supporters were very lively, positive and focused.

As the game kicked off Chelsea dominated possession probing for an opening in the Napoli defence. Daniel Sturridge had an early effort tipped past the post by the 'keeper.

On 12 minutes the Neapolitan side threatened the Chelsea goal when Maggio ran into space and passed only for Cavani to shoot wide.

The early goal had not happened for Chelsea and frustration was starting to creep in, until suddenly a Ramires' cross from the left touchline found Drogba who powered a header into the back of The Shed End net. The fans in the stands erupted. The fuse had been lit.

Before the break Christian Maggio was replaced by former Liverpool man Andrea Dossena. Maybe he had succumbed to an early challenge from Ramires, or maybe the Italian international just could not keep up with the Brazilian's constant running.

In stoppage time David Luiz drove the ball into the six-yard box with pace but Fabio Cannavero stretched to cut it out. In the first minute of the second half Cannavero headed dangerously over bar for a Chelsea corner.

Lampard placed his delivery to the near-post for Terry to run in and flick the perfect header over experienced 'keeper Morgan De Sanctis. The crowd were on their feet and the rapturous cheers could be heard all the way to Putney Bridge. It was 3-3 on aggregate and now Napoli had to score because Chelsea had an away goal.

However, Neapolitan heads did not do down, the Italians increased the pressure on Chelsea's goal and in the 54th minute Gokhan Inler controlled a headed clearance from Terry and coolly placed the ball past Petr Cech. Now Chelsea needed to strike back.

Fernando Torres came on for Daniel Sturridge, Ivanovic had a shot blocked and Drogba drew the save of the night when he hammered a volley toward De Sanctis. Naples attacked in numbers and the Chelsea defending became somewhat desperate.

It was end to end stuff now as the players tired. Chelsea had a succession of corners with scrambles in the six-yard box. It was a question of who could hold their nerve the longest. Then Naples cracked.

Dossena clearly handled an Ivanovic header and German referee Felix Brych pointed to the spot. Lampard cracked the penalty home to make the score 4-4 on aggregate.

The game opened up and the action was not for the faint-hearted as challenges came in hard and fast. There were half-chances at both ends and a Drogba claim for another penalty before the clock ticked to 90 minutes.

As extra-time began Chelsea's aerial bombardment continued with a header from Ivanovic going wide. Florent Malouda and Jose Bosingwa came on for Juan Mata and Terry, who was injured.

Napoli goalkeeper De Sanctis had generally performed well but he misjudged a long punt from Drogba, running under it to allow Torres in behind him, only to see the Spaniard defeated by the angle.

However, a minute before the break Drogba did turn provider. In a congested attack he found some space for a low cross and Serbian Ivanovic smashed the ball into the net from 12 yards. Houston we have lift off! The old stadium shook to its rafters as Chelsea went ahead again.

In the second period of extra time the tension was palpable. Chelsea tried to keep calm, but one goal for Napoli would swing the tie back to the Italians. The result was on a knife-edge. Drogba could have made it safe with a minute to go but volleyed wide.

As the referee blew the final whistle four goals had been enough. The Mighty Blues were through to a Champions League quarter-final with Benfica. They had indeed gone, 'One Step Beyond'.

Drogba said, 'The atmosphere in the stadium was amazing, it made a big difference. We've had some great nights here, but this was one of the best.'

And Lampard added, 'You saw a great spirit in the team, the desire, there were people with cramp running at the end and putting their bodies on the line.'

Ivanovic refused to attribute his winner to the defeat of Napoli, instead opting to praise the team's overall performance.

The Serbian scored the decisive fourth goal against the Italian club in the first-half of extra-time, putting Chelsea 4-1 up on the night. His crucial strike meant that Roberto Di Matteo's men qualified for the quarter-finals with an aggregate score of 5-4.

Yet, despite having scored only three Champions League goals for the club since arriving in 2008, the 28-year-old insisted that the team as a whole should take the plaudits and said the result could act as a springboard for the rest of the season.

Ivanovic told the club's official website, 'It was a crucial game of our season and we started well and scored, which gave us extra confidence.

'It was difficult after we conceded the goal but we got another and played like a team and showed character. This kind of game can change our season.

'It doesn't matter who scored and how isn't important, but it can change a lot of things for the team and give us extra confidence. All the team is very happy to qualify for the next round.'

The defender also played down any suggestion of unrest in the Stamford Bridge camp when he said the team were always focused and positive that they could win the game.

He added, 'We felt before the game we could do this, and came into the game very strong.'

'The big guys know how to play these games and we are strong on these days, everybody can see this and we have to try to stay at this level in the next period.'

'We were two goals down from the first-leg and knew what we had to do. We played like a team and gave everything to qualify for the next round. It was very difficult but everybody is happy because we did it.'

Chelsea made it through to the last 16 tie against Naples with a few hiccups at the group stage.

On matchday one we had a comfortable 2-0 win against Bayer Leverkusen at The Bridge with Mata scoring the second in the 90+2 minute. However, the away fixture at the BayArena ended in a 2-1 defeat thanks to a cruel 90th minute strike from Manuel Friedrich after Drogba had put Chelsea 1-0 up in the first half.

Chelsea were 5-0 winners at home to Genk, courtesy of Raul Meireles, Torres 2, Ivanovic and Kalou, but only managed a 1-1 draw in the away game at the Cristal Arena with a Ramires strike after 25 minutes.

At the Mestalla stadium in Valencia a Lampard penalty earned the Blues a 1-1 draw but a 3-0 win at Stamford Bridge on Matchday 6 saw the Blues cruise through to the clash with Napoli.

GOAL 12
Hazard heroics in battle of The Bridge

Premier League. Chelsea 2-2 Tottenham Hotspur.
8pm Monday, 02-05-2016. Stamford Bridge.
Attendance, 41,545. Eden Hazard (83)

Team: Asmir Begovic, Branislav Ivanovic, Gary Cahill, John Terry, Cesar Azpilicueta, John Obi Mikel, Nemanja Matic (Oscar 78), Willian, Cesc Fabregas, Pedro (Eden Hazard 45), Diego Costa.

A WONDER goal from Eden Hazard saw Chelsea fight back from 0-2 down to shatter Tottenham's title dreams at Stamford Bridge.

Substitute Hazard scored seven minutes from time to complete the comeback and hand Leicester City a historic Premiership crown.

Spurs' only hope of a first top-flight title since 1961 was to win their final three games of the season. Harry Kane and Son Heung-min netted in the 35th and 44th minutes to put them two goals up.

Tempers boiled over in this volatile encounter just before half-time when Danny Rose and Willian had to be pulled apart before Mousa Dembele appeared to gouge Diego Costa's eye. Indeed, Spurs were shown 9 yellow cards – the most by a single team in Premier League history.

Tottenham knew they needed all three points but had not won at Stamford Bridge for 26 years when Gary Lineker scored the winner.

Chelsea boosted by the introduction of Hazard at half-time were right back in the game in the 58th minute thanks to Gary Cahill's opportunist strike in a crowded six-yard area.

That left a nervous 32 minutes for Spurs and Leicester, whose players watched the game at the home of the newly crowned Football

Writers' Player of the Year, Jamie Vardy. And they would have been celebrating as Hazard curled in a sublime equaliser from outside the left-hand corner of the penalty area, leaving 'keeper Hugo Lloris grasping at air.

At the beginning of the season the odds for Leicester winning the first title in their 132-year history were 5000-1. However, manager Claudio Ranieri did show belief in his team by having a bonus for winning the League written into his contract in July.

A great deal had been made of Chelsea's desire to end Spurs' title hopes before kick-off and unsurprisingly Guus Hiddink's side roared into action with Cahill, back in the side with John Terry, heading Cesc Fabregas' corner wide of the post.

Spurs survived Chelsea's opening attacks and had a chance of their own as Rose shot from distance but Asmir Begovic watched on as the ball sailed high over the crossbar.

In a lively affair, John Obi Mikel and Dembele squared up to each other before Kyle Walker appeared to kick out at Pedro after the little Italian winger had gone to ground.

Fabregas fired wide in the 27th minute after excellent work from Costa and minutes later referee Mark Clattenburg gave the first yellow card of the night to Rose after another coming together with Pedro.

In the 29th minute Spurs came close with Kane finding Son at the back post, but the South Korea international struck his shot wide.

Spurs took the lead in the 35th minute when Kane, put through by Erik Lamela, perfectly timed his run and rounded Chelsea 'keeeper Begovic for his 25th League goal of the season.

They were soon two goals up when Son, replacing the suspended Dele Alli, was put through by Christian Eriksen, to slot home in the 44th minute. However, despite Tottenham's two goal advantage players began to lose their cool.

Rose and Willian squared up near the touchline before the break and Spurs' boss Mauricio Pochettino stepped onto the pitch to trigger the arrival of the blue and white hordes.

It was not the last time both sets of players tussled. Television replays showed Dembele's fingers making contact with Costa's eye, but on this occasion he escaped punishment from the referee.

At the break it was the introduction of Hazard for Pedro that changed Chelsea's fortunes. But, Tottenham did keep coming forward with Kane's low shot saved by Begovic before Son fired wide.

Chelsea seemed energised by the deft-skills of Hazard, who cut in from the left flank in the 52nd minute, firing a low shot towards the bottom corner which Lloris saved.

Six minutes later the Blues were right back in it as Cahill brought down Willian's corner before firing a left-footed shot which nestled in the back of the net.

Chelsea were in the ascendency as Willian's curled effort was saved and Pochettino responded by bringing on Ryan Mason for goal scorer Son.

Hazard continued to cause major problems for the visitors, dominating midfield and conjuring chances. Spurs' needed Walker to turn the Belgium international's low cross away to safety.

However, Hazard's brilliant goal was the coup de grace, curling a first time shot into the top-right corner for his first goal at Stamford Bridge since his strike against Crystal Palace the previous year, which secured the title for the Blues.

The goal sparked unbridled joy in the stands for the Stamford Bridge faithful and disbelief in the corner for away fans as they made their way to the exits.

Tottenham's frustrations boiled over in six minutes of added time with Kane and Mason both booked for reckless challenges, and unsavoury scenes continued at the final whistle.

Before the game Hazard told the BBC's Match of the Day, 'The fans, the club, the players, we don't want Tottenham to win the Premier League.

'We hope for Leicester because they deserve to be champions this season. We have a good game against Tottenham and if we beat them it can be good.' After the match midfielder Fabregas said, 'That's why we love this sport so much, it was a fantastic second half and I think everyone enjoyed it. It's a little bit how our season has gone – first half not too good, a little bit too easy. Then a wake-up call and we start performing.

'It's a shame because I believe we have a lot of quality in this team and we can do a lot better. They scored two goals because we didn't defend well enough but I think 70-75 per cent of the game was ours.'

Leicester boss, Claudio Ranieri, said, 'It's an amazing feeling and I'm so happy for everyone. I'm a pragmatic man – I just wanted to win match after match. Never did I think too much about where it would take us.'

Hazard's fine goal against Spurs was one of 85 he scored for Chelsea in 245 Premier League appearances. He was born in 1991 in Belgium but began his playing career with Lille in the French Ligue 1.

In June 2012 he signed for Chelsea and during his years with the Blues he won the UEFA Europa League twice, the Premier League twice, the FA Cup and the League Cup. In 2019 he joined Real Madrid.

Consistently the target of foul play during his time in the Premier League he is calm about the problem, 'I've always been small, so defenders have always been taller and tougher than me. So that's difficult for me. They foul me sometimes, but there you are, that's what the rules of the game are for.

'I have always thought if there is a game and there have been lots of fouls on me, then I have been playing well for the team,' he added. 'You can win a free-kick when there's a foul and that's a chance to score a goal.

'That's my mentality. Just because somebody has fouled me, there is no reason for me to be nasty to him.'

Hazard has also rejected the notion of a shift in the balance of power in London resulting from the opening of Tottenham's new stadium, pointing to Chelsea's seasoned status as trophy winners.

He also pointed to the quality of youngsters including Tammy Abraham and Callum Hudson-Odoi currently emerging from the Chelsea ranks.

'Callum has great skills. If he wants to ask me about something I will tell him, no problem, but he is a great player already. If he wants some advice I can teach him, but you know, he has everything. When you are young you just play,' said Hazard.

'Sometimes you try and miss, but the good thing is to give freshness in the team. Callum can play three games in one week, he has the legs for 90 minutes. At 29, like me, we are a bit tired but he is still young. He can still improve, but he is in a good team to learn and we are happy to help him.'

Hazard's style of play and his commitment to the game apart, it is of course his goals that hit the headlines.

Another sublime piece of footballing skill came in the London derby between Chelsea and Arsenal in February 2017.

Hazard picked the ball up just inside his own half and set off towards goal. He swerved away from Laurent Koscielny, held off Coquelin and continued his run. Koscielny got back but Hazard wriggled past him in the area and hit the ball over Cech from close range. Pure genius.

GOAL 11
Cole shines for back-to-back titles

Premier League. Chelsea 3-0 Man. United.

Saturday, 29-4-2000 at Stamford Bridge.

Attendance, 42,219. Joe Cole (61)

Team: Petr Cech, Paulo Ferreira, Ricardo Carvalho, John Terry, William Gallas, Claude Makelele, Joe Cole (Crespo 76), Michel Essien, Frank Lampard, Arjen Robben (Duff 66), Didier Drogba (Maniche 85).

A UNIQUE goal from Camden-born Joe Cole helped Chelsea clinch a second successive Premiership title with victory over Manchester United at Stamford Bridge.

Boyhood Chelsea fan Cole was inspired, a constant problem for Gary Neville, his display crowned with the goal that made sure this would be a Blue Day. In midfield Claude Makelele's intelligent performance showed why Chelsea are ahead of the game compared with the visitors.

Jose Mourinho's Blues needed only one more point to secure another title and William Gallas set them on their way with a fifth minute strike. Joe Cole added a brilliant individual goal on the hour and Ricardo Carvalho hit home Chelsea's third.

Before the game Cole said, 'We want to win it at home. It will be a fantastic season with back-to-back titles which has not been done by Chelsea before.

'When I'm playing regularly, I feel happy and that's when I get my strength and power to go past someone, which is so important to me.'

Mourinho restored Cole and Arjen Robben to the side that narrowly lost the FA Cup semi-final 2-1 against Liverpool. Cole came on as substitute at Old Trafford, missing a golden chance to square the match.

'That miss will haunt me, but there you go,' he said. 'We just didn't get going and we take collective responsibility for that. But this will make us all the more determined to go out against Manchester United and win the title.'

Mourinho said, 'I told the players before the match we can't allow a team to come here and take away the trophy. It's ours. We deserve it.'

And with only a point needed to put the seal on another title triumph, Chelsea made the ideal start when they went ahead with only five minutes on the clock.

Frank Lampard's corner was knocked forward by Didier Drogba and Gallas darted in to head past the bemused Edwin Van der Sar. On the bench Mourinho sat expressionless as around him Stamford Bridge erupted.

There was a major scare for Chelsea and England two minutes later when John Terry was felled by a late tackle from international team-mate Wayne Rooney.

The Chelsea captain lay motionless for several minutes but, just as a stretcher was called out, he recovered and was able to continue after several minutes' treatment.

Rooney was United's main threat and he almost capped a solo run with an equaliser after 21 minutes but pulled his shot wide with only Petr Cech to beat. And he brought another fine save from the big 'keeper just before half-time, Cech diving low to his right to save Rooney's strong 20-yard-strike.

In the second half Cole launched a skillful attempt to put the game beyond United's reach with an audacious chip, but the ball drifted wide of the far post.

However, after 61 minutes Cech's enormous throw was chested down by Drogba for Cole. The Chelsea man tricked his way past Rio Ferdinand, Nemanja Vidic and Mikel Silvestre before racing on to fire high past Van der Sar. This time Mourinho jumped up, shaking his fists in celebration.

Desperate United manager Sir Alex Ferguson made a change after

64 minutes, Sending on Ruud van Nistelrooy for the disappointing Christiano Ronaldo.

By then the mortal wounds had been delivered but Carvalho was hungry for more, beginning and ending a sweeping move for Mourinho's team. The Portugal defender, helped along by Lampard and Cole, caressed a swerving right-foot shot that nestled inside the near post. 'Boring, boring Chelsea,' chorused the faithful in the Matthew Harding stand.

Rooney was then involved in an incident that cast a shadow over England's World Cup plans with 15 minutes left. He stumbled into an innocuous challenge with Paulo Ferreira, but collapsed clutching the same right foot he broke against Portugal in Euro 2004.

The England striker looked in agony as he was strapped on to a stretcher, leaving the field to sympathetic applause from fans of both sides.

Chelsea's title party started in earnest as referee Mike Dean, from Wirral, blew the final whistle, but on a day of glory Cole shone with a stylish display and superb solo goal.

Mourinho said, 'The result of the game perhaps does not reflect how well Manchester United played.

'They really made it tough for us and were fantastic with their attacking movement.

'But we overcame it to confirm our position as Premiership champions.'

Manchester United boss Sir Alex Ferguson said, 'It was harsh and I don't think 3-0 was a fair reflection of our performance.

'If you lose goals as softly as we did today you have to take your medicine for that.

'We had a lot of the play and made some good chances but we didn't make it count.

'But Chelsea deserve all the plaudits they will get and especially on their home form, they are worthy champions.'

The second title victory was one of the highlights of Cole's time at

Stamford Bridge. The 22-year-old was signed for £6.6 million from West Ham in 2003 soon after Roman Abramovich bought Chelsea.

Although Cole had been training with West Ham since he was eight-years-old, the affinity he had with his new club immediately showed with the fans who took to him as one of their own.

He made his debut coming off the bench against MSK Zilina in a Champions League qualifier and played a part in Chelsea's second goal. Under Claudio Ranieri many of Cole's appearances were from the subs' bench and when Mourinho took over in 2004 he was in and out of the team.

'It certainly crossed my mind maybe I wasn't going to make it at Chelsea and I might have to move on,' he said in 2005. 'I didn't want to go because I've always been very happy at this club. But you have to look after your career, I wasn't getting the chances I felt I deserved.

'There were a lot of frustrating times when I'd be sitting on the bench and thinking I could be out there contributing. There was interest from other clubs but I decided to stay and it was the right choice.'

Cole underlined his affinity with younger supporters and the future of the club when he said, 'The club have got to find a way of filling the ground. The normal fan cannot afford the prices. We have to attract a new generation of fans to come to Stamford Bridge.'

He has also expressed strong views on diving and simulation, 'There are some players in this country who are divers but I'm not one of them. I would never dive.

'It was frustrating for me to be accused of diving because we've not had many dribbling players in this country for a few years.

'Sometimes you run at such a high speed that if you get clipped you go flying. It can look like a dive but that's misleading because it's never intentional.'

England manager Sven Goran Eriksson said in 2006, 'Cole is the most improved England player of the last year. He has been in every squad that I have picked if fit.

'That is because I believe in him and the ability he has. Even when he wanted to do too many tricks in the wrong places and at the wrong time, I've always persevered.'

Cole also came to the attention of Pele the world's most iconic ex-player, 'The number 10 for Chelsea, Joe Cole, is a very good player and when I saw him in the first half against Charlton he was excellent.

'He has the skills of a Brazilian but he needs to learn when to show the skills and when to play the simple game.

'In the second half, when the game was very close, he kept losing the ball because he was trying too hard and Chelsea nearly lost the game. The tricks are fine at 3-0 or 4-0 but not at 0-0 or 1-1.

'That's why Ronaldinho is so good, he knows when do the tricks and when to keep it simple. When I was playing and it was 0-0 we would keep the ball and pass it around.'

Finally, a story from Neil 'Spy' Barnett who quotes Peter Brabrook, a Chelsea contemporary of Jimmy Greaves and later a West Ham schoolboy and youth coach.

'Joe Cole was the best schoolboy and youth player I've ever seen. He was better than Jimmy Greaves. Jimmy scored goals. Joe had more to his game,' said Brabrook.

'He was unbelievable on the ball. He did more tricks than Tommy Cooper. That goes away as you go up the levels, but he retained an element of it and still has it today.'

GOAL 10
Terry buries Barca in 'greatest game'

UEFA Champions League. Chelsea 4-2 Barcelona.
(First-leg 1-2. Chelsea win 5-4 on agg)
Tuesday, 08-03-2005 at Stamford Bridge.
Attendance, 41,515. John Terry (76)

Team: Petr Cech, Paulo Ferreira (Glen Johnson 51), Ricardo Carvalho, John Terry, William Gallas, Claude Makelele, Joe Cole, Frank Lampard, Damien Duff (Robert Huth 85), Mateja Kezman, Eidur Gudjohnsen (Tiago 78).

FOR many supporters John Terry exemplifies what supporting Chelsea is all about, pride, grit, passion and overcoming adversity whatever the odds.

Jimmy Greaves said, 'He may be one of the most controversial players in the history of the British game for non-footballing reasons, but John Terry has been one of its most reliable and consistent performers out there on the pitch.

'A defender's defender, unbelievably solid with such a none-shall-pass attitude, Terry has been the captain and lynchpin of Chelsea's recent golden years.'

In this last 16 encounter, Terry led his team out to face Barcelona at a bursting Stamford Bridge as 'Blue Is The Colour' boomed from the stadium speakers.

Barcelona kicked off leading 2-1 on aggregate from the first-leg. Chelsea won a free-kick near the sideline halfway into the Barcelona half. Frank Lampard looped it into the box, the goalkeeper flapped at it and Barca won a free-kick for a nudge on Victor Valdes by Mateja

Kezman. Moments later Chelsea attacked on the break after excellent defending by Ricardo Carvalho who sent Eidur Gudjohnsen on his way. He released Kezman but a very late flag from the linesman stopped his sprint into the final third. An excellent start by the Blues, the visitors looked vulnerable to both those early attacks.

After seven minutes Gudjohnsen put Chelsea ahead, rifling the ball home from about 10 yards after he controlled a low, first-time Kezman cross from the right wing. He turned and took it past Presas Oleguer before hitting his shot past 'keeper Valdes.

The Bridge was buzzing after brilliant play from the two strikers and a great start for Chelsea.

As play went on Frank Rijkaard leaned against the dugout with a pained look on his face as he watched Joe Cole win a corner from Giovanni van Bronkhorst. Damian Duff sent the ball into the box and John Terry flicked the in-swinger to Frank Lampard who volleyed a good chance over the crossbar. It could have been 2-0.

Duff slipped in behind the Barcelona defence but his cross from the left didn't quite find Kezman. The Barca defence was really creaking with some gaping holes appearing for Chelsea to exploit.

Barcelona eased the pressure by winning a free kick 35 yards out, straight in front of the Chelsea goal. Deco lofted the ball towards Andres Iniesta just outside the six-yard box but Chelsea cleared the danger.

Chelsea continued to press and after 16 minutes Cole picked up the ball on the right wing and beat van Bronkhorst. The subsequent cross was deflected towards Valdes who could only parry into the path of Lampard who smashed his shot past the stricken keeper. It was 2-0, Chelsea were 3-2 up on aggregate.

Two minutes later it was 3-0 as Duff picked up a through-ball, ran at Valdes and slotted the ball home through his legs. Chelsea were in dreamland, The Bridge a seething cauldron of noise as everyone tried to process exactly what was happening.

After 22 minutes Samuel Eto'o shot from outside the Chelsea box but Cech tipped his rising effort over the bar. From the corner Roberto

Carvalho allowed Ronaldinho a free header which was just a foot wide of the near post.

Then reality bit. The linesman drew referee Pierluigi Collina's attention to a handball by Ferreira in the box. He'd jumped for a header while waving his arms and clearly hit the ball. Ronaldinho put away the penalty for 3-1.

After 30 minutes a slight lull, there had been four goals, great attacking, poor defending and a spectrum of emotions and there was still an hour to go.

Barcelona started to control the middle of the pitch so Chelsea manager Jose Mourinho pulled Gudjohnson back into midfield, allowing Lampard to play in front of Makelele and Terry where Barca looked most dangerous.

After 37 minutes Cech made a great save from a Deco free-kick taken about 35 yards out.

Just one minute later Ronaldinho scored an unbelievable goal to make it 3-2. He was on the edge of the D of Chelsea's penalty area and he wrong-footed three Blues' defenders with a wave of his boot behind the ball prodding it to the left of Cech with a shot that had no back-lift whatsoever. Chelsea needed to score again. Barcelona were now totally in charge with the scores level on aggregate and two away goals to their credit.

In the final minute of the half Chelsea responded with a furious attack on the Barca goal only to see a Cole shot crash off the upright. With Valdes lying helplessly on the ground the ball was just out of the reach of the incoming Duff who stretched but could only caress the ball weakly into the 'keeper's chest.

In the second half Barcelona stroked the ball around the field, defying the Blues to come and get it from them. They seemed to have renewed confidence and Cech had to save low from Juliano Belletti before producing a brilliant low save from Carles Puyol's header.

When Chelsea won a free kick 40 yards from Barcelona's goal, Lampard stepped up and hit the ball with such force it flew like an Exocet missile inches past Valdes' left upright. With 20 minutes left Chelsea still needed another goal. After zipping around the Barca penalty area, the ball dropped for Gudjohnsen on the angle of the six-yard box but his shot was blocked by Belletti.

In the Chelsea half Iniesta beat Duff and William Gallas on the left and cut inside to shoot, but Cech managed to touch his effort on to the post. Glen Johnson was slow to react and with the goal gaping Eto'o blasted the ball over the bar. What a let-off.

With 15 minutes left Duff sent in a corner and Terry leapt highest and strongest sending the ball in at the unguarded far post. It was 4-2 to Chelsea on the night and 5-4 on aggregate. Now Barcelona had to score to stay in the Champions League.

In the stands there was total mayhem. The small band of Barca supporters sat in silence as total pandemonium erupted around them. There was real belief in the side now. Chelsea could do this, but it would be a nervous last 15 minutes.

After 81 minutes Lampard caught Deco napping and tried to dink the ball over Puyol's head to release Kezman. Puyol did just enough to intercept the pass which would have left Kezman through with just the 'keeper to beat.

With four minutes to go Barcelona had a corner but Terry was fouled by Gerard and won a free kick. The Barcelona pressure was relentless and there would be three minutes of added time.

With everyone forward for Barca, Chelsea broke but Lampard sensibly took the ball into the corner to waste some time.

Barca won a free kick outside the Chelsea box but Deco thumped it across the face of goal and two yards wide of the far post.

Ninety-three minutes and it was all over, Chelsea were through to the quarter-finals of the Champions League. Captain Terry had been magnificent and it was his headed goal that has taken Chelsea through in one of the greatest games ever.

Terry was born in Barking, London in December 1980 and was regarded as one of the best defenders in the world at his peak captaining

Chelsea and England. As an inspirational 'captain, leader, legend' during his long career with the club JT built great rapport with the fans and a reputation that he would risk life and limb if it helped the team.

He was Chelsea's most successful captain, leading the Blues to five Premier League titles, four FA Cups, three League Cups, one UEFA Europa League and one UEFA Champions League title.

He was named UEFA Club Defender of the Year in 2005, 2008 and 2009 and included in the FIFPro World XI for five consecutive years from 2005-2009.

Carlo Ancelotti said, 'John Terry is the captain of all team captains, he was born with the captain's armband on his arm. Even without the band it is as if he wears it anyway... he works twice as hard as everybody else.'

Talking about Chelsea's tremendous away support Terry said, 'Often it feels like we are at a home match when we have so many fans there. The singing, the cheering really helps the players.'

Terry also had immense praise for his former manager Jose Mourinho, 'When he told us something, that we were going to win 4-0 or 5-0, it always happened. Always, it was like he could predict the future. When he said we need more champions in the dressing room to become better, I just believed everything he said.

'He was the best manager and the best coach as well. He did everything. He was the one who came and revolutionised Chelsea. He would be the first in at 8am, he would be the one setting the cones out and he'd be out there, if it was pouring with rain, getting his session organised.'

Mourinho still keeps in touch with his former Chelsea captain and has monitored the way his managerial career has progressed with Aston Villa. He said it is based on different experiences, being an assistant, going to the Championship, leaving the Championship, coming to the premier League and taking his time.

'His moment to grow up and reach what he wants to reach will arrive, so I am really proud of the way he is doing things,' said Mourinho.

And the final word goes to Ray Parlour, often an opponent with Arsenal against Terry's Chelsea, 'John Terry, he wears his shirt on his sleeve.'

GOAL 9
Wise's fabulous goal at the San Siro

UEFA Champions League. AC Milan 1-1 Chelsea.

Tuesday, 26-10-1999 at Stadio San Siro, Milan.

Attendance, 74,855. Dennis Wise (77)

Team: Ed de Goey, Albert Ferrer, Marcel Desailly, Frank Leboeuf, Celestine Babayaro, Dan Petrescu (Jody Morris 46), Dennis Wise, Didier Deschamps, Gustavo Poyet (Roberto Di Matteo 74), Tore Andre Flo, Gianfranco Zola (Gabriele Ambrosetti 81).

SITTING under an azure sky at a pavement café just yards from the Duomo, the immense gothic cathedral in Milan, life couldn't get much better for three Chelsea boys.

Work on the cathedral started in 1386 and took nearly 600 years to complete, the roofline is famous for its dense grid of pinnacles and spires supported by flying buttresses.

With its 108m spire it is the largest Gothic cathedral in the world, a fusion of Gothic and Renaissance styles. While my two intrepid companions disappeared to climb the 250 steps to the Duomo rooftop terrace, I decided to take it easy.

In the autumnal sunlight with ice cold beers at hand I watched the world go by and waited for the evening's match between AC Milan and Chelsea.

The memory of the game itself has a certain dreamlike quality for the author as I had caught an early flight from Gatwick having worked as a newspaper sub-editor until 1.30am, then headed straight for the airport.

The match was a triumph for Chelsea manager Gianluca Vialli, proving his Italian detractors wrong with an important Champions League draw against European giants AC Milan.

A wonderful late equaliser from volatile captain Dennis Wise left Chelsea needing only a draw with group leaders Hertha Berlin to progress to the competition's second round.

It was a huge European performance from the Blues. Chelsea's line-up displayed all their passion and talent as they forced the Italian club onto the back foot from kick-off.

Norwegian striker Tore Andre Flo never stopped running as Chelsea launched wave after wave of attacks from all quarters.

From the way the game opened, it was obvious Vialli and his many former Serie A clubmates were desperate for victory on their return to Italian soil.

There was never any danger of the game turning into a stale European encounter, with Milan believing they needed no less than victory to keep their Champions League hopes alive.

Flo had scored twice against Galatasaray and the Milan defence boxed him in whenever it could.

However, he still managed to find space but wasted several first half chances including a virtual open goal when he arrived in the six-yard box to meet a Wise cross but he shot over the bar.

Chelsea's defence kept a tight rein on Milan's top scorer Andriy Shevchenko but he too managed to cause problems.

A first-half free kick looked goal bound but swung just wide of the left-hand post. Shevchenko actually beat De Goey but the ball crashed against the left-hand post.

De Goey made a crucial save eight minutes into the second half when he flew to his right to tip a Massimo Ambrosini volley round the post.

Three minutes later Oliver Bierfhoff looked to have worked himself clear of the Chelsea defence as the ball came to him on the far post – but he put his header over the bar.

The match was played at a frantic pace, stoked by the thick red firecracker smoke which swirled around the home supporters at the San Siro.

Milan looked more composed after the break but Chelsea continued to probe for that vital goal.

The Blues refused to compromise their attacking style and with 22 minutes to go looked to have been rewarded when Gus Poyet darted between two defenders to find himself with a simple header from six yards out. Unfortunately, he directed it straight at Milan 'keeper Christian Abbiati.

Seconds later the miss looked to have proved fatal when Bierfhoff beat Frank Leboeuf to a near-post cross and edged the ball past De Goey to put Milan ahead.

Urged on by their huge and vocal away support Chelsea refused to be subdued and four minutes later grabbed an equaliser in emphatic fashion.

Roberto Di Matteo, on as substitute in place of the injured Gus Poyet, hit a looping high ball over the Milan back four which Wise controlled with the touch of a born-striker, and then clipped under the body of the advancing Abbiati.

Vialli, usually the most conservative of managers, exploded from the touchline in a picture of jubilation.

With ten minutes remaining news came through that Galatasaray were leading Hertha Berlin 3-1. The news meant Milan only needed a draw if they beat the Turks in their final game and the Italians seemed to ease down a gear.

Chelsea were happy with the draw and only needed a point from their final game with Hertha Berlin which they won 2-0 at Stamford Bridge.

The European adventure continued for Chelsea in the second group phase with fine performances against Feyenoord, SS Lazio and Olympique de Marseille earning a quarter-final place against FC Barcelona.

Gianluca Vialli's team won a memorable first-leg at Stamford Bridge 3-1 with two goals from Tore Andre Flo and a strike from Gianfranco Zola. However following an epic second-leg at the Camp Nou watched by 97,000 fans Chelsea finally succumbed 5-1 after extra-time with Flo scoring once again for the Blues who exited the competition losing 6-4 on aggregate.

Dennis Wise was born in West London on December 16, 1966. He said, 'The area of London I grew up in, around Shepherd's Bush and Notting Hill, was tough. Basically, you had to learn to look after yourself.

'It doesn't help if you are accident prone, which is exactly how I would describe myself. Not clumsy but if anything was going to happen it would happen to me. If someone was going to get knocked down by an ice-cream van it would be Dennis Wise. If anyone was going to fall off a tree in the park, it would be me.'

He was a member of the infamous 'Crazy Gang' at Wimbledon that reached the FA Cup final in 1988 and helped his side defeat heavy favourites Liverpool 2-1.

Wise signed for Chelsea in July, 1990, for a then club record fee of £1.6 million, scored 13 goals in 44 matches as Chelsea finished the season in 11th place. Wise's former Wimbledon teammate Vinnie Jones joined Chelsea prior to the 1991-92 season and the intimidating presence of his fellow Londoner in midfield seemed to help him rediscover his best form.

Wise was Chelsea's top scorer for the season with 14 goals from midfield, with perhaps his best performance coming in a 2-1 victory away to Liverpool in February 1992.

Chelsea's first FA Cup final in 24 years was a disappointing 4-0 defeat to Manchester United but Wise soon captained the team to the final again in the 2-0 victory over Middlesbrough in 1997.

The fiery midfielder, always a fans' favourite but often a menace for referees, led Chelsea to another 2-0 victory over Middlesbrough the following season, this time in the League Cup Final.

He also captained Chelsea in the Cup Winners Cup Final, a dinked pass over the Stuttgart defence setting up Gianfranco Zola to score the winner, moments after coming on as substitute.

Wise said, 'We knew for certain that Stuttgart would be a strong and disciplined side. I never thought for one minute that it would be a classic match. We expected the Germans to soak up the pressure and hit us on the break.

'When Franco came on for Tore I spotted the space he had made for himself and just played the ball through. Franco took one touch and produced a fantastic finish. It was world-class to produce that kind of skill and show that composure after being on the field for such a short while.'

After his adventures in the Champions League, Wise steered Chelsea to their second FA Cup win in three years, this time courtesy of a Roberto Di Matteo goal in a 1-0 victory over Aston Villa in 2000.

With new manager Claudio Ranieri seeking to lower the age of his Chelsea squad, he was sold to Leicester City in June 2001 for £1.6 million.

Wise said, 'I had 11 wonderful years at Stamford Bridge. I'll always class it as my home. I'm sorry I had to leave.'

Television football commentator Martin Tyler said, 'The ageless Dennis Wise, now in his thirties…'

And the then chairman, Ken Bates, told the tale, 'We had our best player of the year dance as supporters elected Wise their Player Of The Year. Dennis accepted his award mimicking Vialli, whereupon Zola shouted 'speak English', Dennis switched to his normal cockney voice only for Zola to shout 'you're still not speaking English'.'

However, the then Manchester United manager, Sir Alex Ferguson, commenting on Chelsea's Wise said, 'He could start a row in an empty house.'

Many long-term supporters of the Blues understand that all these sentiments don't quite fully sum up this complex Chelsea legend.

GOAL 8
Unbelievable Torres stuns Barcelona

UEFA CL semi-final, 2nd leg. Barcelona 2-2 Chelsea.
(Chelsea win 3-2 on aggregate)
Tuesday, 24-04-12 at Camp Nou.
Attendance, 95,845. Fernando Torres (90+1)

Team: Petr Cech, Branislav Ivanovic, Gary Cahill (Jose Bosingwa 12), John Terry, Ashley Cole, Juan Mata (Salomon Kalou 57), Frank Lampard, John Obi Mikel, Raul Meireles, Ramires, Didier Drogba (Fernando Torres 79)

ON a fine evening in Barcelona locals and tourists alike can be found strolling along Las Ramblas, a fine boulevard which runs through the heart of the city.

It offers an eclectic mix of street performers, human statues, portrait artists, caricaturists, mosaics, museums and market stalls.

When Chelsea qualified to play Barca in the semi-final of the Champions League in 2012, Las Ramblas became the hub for thousands of travelling supporters to sample the bars, beer and tapas or stay overnight in one of the many small hotels in the Ravel area or Gothic Quarter.

Chelsea had won a pulsating encounter in the first-leg of the tie at Stamford Bridge 1-0, courtesy of a Didier Drogba goal late in first half injury time. John Terry said, 'Our midfielders had to work really hard as did Didier up front on his own as well. It was a great, tireless performance from everyone.'

In Barcelona the task was going to be even more immense against Messi and Co. a team many pundits had labelled as the best club side in the world. The author and his friends were at the first-leg and decided that they too would chase glory in a Mission to Catalonia.

After many hours of sampling ice cold beverages along Las Ramblas we made our way to the Camp Nou, stopping off at a bar full of friendly Barca supporters to break the journey.

The sheer scale of the stadium was an awe-inspiring sight, reminiscent of the Colosseum in Rome, with ranks of tiny seats placed on ever higher and steeper terracing.

Didier Drogba was passed fit so manager Roberto Di Matteo named the same side as the first-leg.

Petr Cech said, 'I think it will be the same type of game as the first-leg and I hope we can score again. A goal for us is going to make a big difference in terms of the whole game.'

As the match kicked off Chelsea showed good attacking intent as Ashley Cole's pass breached the Barca penalty area within 18 seconds but 'keeper Victor Valdes collected ahead of Ramires.

But then Barcelona attacked and with just two minutes played Messi had his first chance but put it into the side netting from inside the penalty area.

Chelsea defended heroically but there was an early blow in the sixth minute when Gary Cahill was forced off after pulling his hamstring. Jose Boswinga came on and Branislav Ivanovic moved to centre back.

It was soon level on the injury front when the influential Gerard Pique lasted just 26 minutes of his recall after failing to recover from a collision with Valdes.

The pattern of the game was similar to that of the first-leg with resolute Chelsea defending deep and in numbers.

However, within 35 minutes Pep Guardiola's side were back on terms on aggregate after Sergio Busquets hit home. Two minutes later the Blues were in serious trouble when Terry was dismissed for a knee in the back of Alexis Sanchez.

Before the game talk had been dominated by refereeing meltdowns in previous clashes but Terry simply gave the referee no choice but to show him a red card. Worse was to follow when after 44 minutes Andres Iniesta beat Cech to make it 2-0 on the night. It felt like the floodgates were opening.

However, a minute later Ramires grabbed a precious away goal in the final salvo of the first half. Frank Lampard's exquisite through-ball gave the Brazilian an opportunity he did not squander, producing a sublime first-time chip over the Barca 'keeper Valdes from 15 yards.

Chelsea's recovery looked likely to be short-lived when Drogba brought down Cesc Fabregas for a penalty at the start of the second half. Cech stood tall and Lionel Messi missed a glorious opportunity to put Barca back in front by crashing his spot kick against the face of the bar.

After the game Messi remained without a goal against Chelsea in eight matches, the most games he has played against a single opponent without a scoring.

Lampard was lucky to escape punishment for a flare-up with Fabregas, Sanchez nodded substitute Dani Alves' cross wide, and Cech was booked for time-wasting having already been warned before saving well again from Isaac Cuenca.

Ivanovic almost capitalised after Drogba helped Chelsea win a corner but he was warned himself after going down theatrically, while Lampard was fortunate only to see yellow for cutting down Fabregas after Messi was booked for tugging him back.

The 10-man Blues were hanging on and were given two lifelines in 60 seconds in the final 10 minutes when Sanchez had a goal ruled out for offside and a Messi strike hit the post from outside the penalty area.

Now every Barcelona mistake was drawing a frustrated reaction from the crowd and when Chelsea won the ball it would be launched into the open spaces up the field.

Then came substitute Torres' moment of glory. Chelsea had been camped on the edge of their box for huge periods as Barca probed for an opening, but Chelsea's progress to the final was assured in stoppage time.

Torres, who had been back defending, suddenly picked up a long clearance up field from Cole. He was in his own half with no one between him and Valdes. He took the ball on and went past the keeper before slotting in, as he had done so many times in the past against this opposition.

The Blues had produced one of the most memorable Champions League performances in history as they defeated Barcelona 3-2 on aggregate in their semi-final at Camp Nou.

Chelsea displayed massive depths of resolve in defence to stymie the reigning European Champions, playing the majority of the second-leg contest with only ten men after Terry was shown the red card.

The only sour note for the Blues was that suspensions meant they would have to do without Ramires, Terry, Ivanovic and Raul Meireles in the final.

Torres had scored the greatest goal of his career and was one step nearer fulfilling one of his lifetime ambitions.

When he joined the Blues from Liverpool, for a then Premier League club to club record £50million fee, he said, 'I want to say thanks to the Chelsea fans because I have seen them very, very happy with me for joining Chelsea.

'The Champions League is a big ambition and all footballers want to play in it. It is a very important competition.

'The biggest ambition in my career is still to win the European Cup. I want to have a picture of that to look at later, I want to have that medal. You can have a contract that is better than your friends but no player looks back and says, 'I won more money.'

Excitable Sky television pundit Gary Neville helped to immortalise the Torres goal with his lively commentary which went, 'Fernando Torres… [long pause] Aaaaaaagh!'

As he regained some composure he continued, 'Unbelievable, unbelievable. The last 18 months have just been forgotten in those seconds. It's gone absolutely wild. It's a huge, huge moment for Chelsea. A huge moment for English football.'

Manager Di Matteo said, 'It was an incredible game. There were so many events. I am very happy but most of all pleased for the players because they deserve this. They have had a difficult season and they seem to be able to do something special when they need to. This seems to be in the DNA of these players. We seem to be able to find some reserves from somewhere. It's just incredible.'

Torres' goal made him the 19th player in Champions League history to score against Real Madrid and Barcelona, the first Spaniard to do so. Chelsea's 2-2 draw gave them an unbeaten record at the Camp Nou in their last four matches, having drawn all of them.

After the match Lampard said, 'It was a magnificent night for everyone involved with the club; the players, the staff, the fans who have come out here, the fans at home. There's no coincidence in what Robbie's done, he's got players playing, he's created an atmosphere and the camp's very happy. Results don't lie and I can't speak highly enough of him.'

As the dazed but delirious Mission to Catalonia team made their way to the airport and then home again, the events of the day were almost too much to take in. Our minds were buzzing. We had done it, we really had.

Makeshift, ten-man Chelsea had unbelievably held Barcelona at the Camp Nou, scoring two sublime goals with Messi missing a penalty. We were in the Champions League Final, again.

GOAL 7
Gronkjaer conjures Russian revolution

Premier League. Chelsea 2-1 Liverpool.

Saturday, 11-05-2003 at Stamford Bridge.

Attendance, 41,911. Jesper Gronkjaer (26).

Team: Carlo Cudicini, Celestine Babayaro, Marcel Desailly, Frank Lampard, Jimmy Floyd Hasselbaink (Carlton Cole 80), William Gallas, Graeme Le Saux, Mario Melchiot, Emmanuel Petit, Eidur Gudjohnsen (Gianfranco Zola 72), Jesper Gronkjaer (Mario Stanic 68).

THE team above may well be considered the £1billion Blues. They are the players who won the game and qualification for the Champions League which probably persuaded Roman Abramovich to buy Chelsea.

Despite successes on the pitch the club had run into dire financial difficulty. On the final day of the domestic League season Chelsea welcomed Liverpool to The Bridge with both teams fighting for the last available Champions League place.

The national press had dubbed the fixture the £20million match but for Chelsea it was much, much more - the club's future was hanging by a thread.

Before kick-off chief executive Trevor Birch went into the home dressing room to make it clear to the team that if they failed to qualify there would be cost-cutting and reduced wages for many players. The spectre of financial collapse was looming large as fans, players and staff held their breath for the very existence of the club.

At a packed Stamford Bridge, Liverpool obviously hadn't read the script when just 11 minutes into the game, Finland international Sami Hyypia escaped some slack marking to head home Danny Murphy's free kick. The home crowd nevertheless gave huge backing to their team and just three minutes later Jesper Gronkjaer collected the ball on the right, he fired in a cross which was met by Marcel Desailly and the ball nestled in the back of Jerzy Dudek's net.

As the game resumed referee Alan Wiley played a good advantage as Graeme Le Saux was felled by Jamie Carragher, but Chelsea failed to use it as Eidur Gudjohnsen fired over when well placed.

For a team needing to win, Liverpool's attacks carried little conviction and the preferred partnership of Michael Owen and Milan Baros lacked the physical presence to ruffle Desailly and William Gallas.

Liverpool's task took on mountainous proportions on 26 minutes when Gronkjaer fired Chelsea ahead. The Dane collected on the right-hand corner of the penalty area and brushed off John-Arne Riise's weak challenge before curling a delicious shot around Dudek's despairing dive.

Chelsea coach Claudio Ranieri left Gianfranco Zola on the bench and his preferred strike pairing almost combined at the start of the second half, with Gudjohnsen just failing to make contact with Hasselbaink's cross.

Liverpool substitute Emile Heskey had a fierce shot blocked and Owen volleyed Riise's cross over as they looked for a route back in. Steve Gerrard then let fly from 30 yards to bring a good save from Carlo Cudicini.

Liverpool's desperation for a goal risked leaving them short-handed at the back and Djimi Traore twice had to be alert as Chelsea broke quickly.

Liverpool were denied a 77th-minute equaliser by a sharp-eyed linesman who spotted Baros's handball before he slotted the ball home.

Chelsea came within a cat's whisker of a third goal on 84 minutes when Dudek scrambled to push Mario Melchiot's shot on to the post.

Salt was rubbed in Liverpool's wounds when Gerrard was rightly shown a second yellow card for a poor, reckless challenge on Le Saux and headed off for an early bath.

The importance of this result cannot be overstated, as qualification for the Champions League was considered essential to Abramovich's impending takeover of the club. Looking back at the match Grønkjaer said, 'I remember the goal very well. I was on the right wing when we got a throw-in, but instead of passing I cut in from the right before sticking it in the other corner. It was a nice feeling, and a good reward for a great season.'

Grønkjaer was born in Denmark on August 12, 1977, he was a pacey winger who played mainly on the right or left wing, or as a second striker. He played a total of 400 League games for a number of European clubs, most notably playing more than 100 games for Chelsea and winning the 1999 Dutch Cup with Ajax Amsterdam. Grønkjaer ended his career with FC Copenhagen, winning four Danish Superliga titles with the club.

In October 2000, Grønkjaer joined Chelsea for £7.8 million from Ajax, which made him at that time the most expensive Danish football player. However, he was side-lined with an injury until January 2001. His career at Chelsea lasted four years although his form during that time was inconsistent.

At his best he was a threat creating and scoring some very important goals for the club. In Chelsea's fourth round FA Cup match away to Gillingham on January 28, 2001, Grønkjaer started his first match for the club and impressed as he scored two goals and hit the post twice, as Chelsea won 4-2.

In the 2003-04 UEFA Champions League quarter-final second-leg away at Highbury, Grønkjaer came on for Scott Parker in the second-half, with Arsenal leading 1-0 on the night and 2-1 on aggregate.

Within six minutes of the substitution, Chelsea equalised through a goal by Frank Lampard. Wayne Bridge scored three minutes before the final whistle and Chelsea went on to defeat Arsenal 3-2 on aggregate and book a place in the semi-finals.

In the semi-final against AS Monaco, Gronkjaer scored from outside the penalty area with a cross-come-shot, but it was not enough for Chelsea to reach the final as the Blues were defeated 5-3 on aggregate.

Grønkjaer also scored at Old Trafford against Manchester United in the penultimate game of the 2003-04 season, the second of a three-game scoring streak. His final goal for Chelsea came the following week against Leeds United, where he scored the winner with a header in the first half.

However, it is the goal against Liverpool that has become legendary as one of the most important in the club's history, as it paved the way for the Russian revolution.

However, in fact Chelsea only needed to avoid defeat against Liverpool to guarantee Champions League football, so it was Marcel Desailly's header to equalise Sami Hyypia's opener rather than Gronkjaer's winner which should really be feted as the key moment.

That has not stopped it becoming fixed in the collective memory of supporters, though – and it was a great goal, worthy of its legendary status. The winger skipped past John Arne Riise and fired low past Jerzy Dudek in the 26th minute of the match; weeks later Abramovich bought the club. The simplicity of the chain of events is too good to resist.

Gronkjaer remembers, 'It was a massive game for Chelsea. We all knew what we were playing for. I remember the stories about our financial situation.'

Beating Liverpool put catastrophe on hold, and on July 1, Abramovich slapped his £140million down on the table. Gronkjaer's contribution was lost in a frenzy of spending as a whole new team was bought before the transfer window closed – a chaotic situation that he recalls was very unsettling for the players who were already at the club.

'I was on holiday in Denmark in my summer house when I heard about the takeover. I didn't imagine Abramovich would have so much money and everything would change. No one did,' Gronkjaer said.

'I remember on the second day of pre-season Abramovich turned up at the training ground and spoke to us in Russian, with someone translating. There were rumours about everything – new coach, new players, new training ground, new stadium.

'He wanted us all to calm down. It was a stressful period for everyone, and the players had mixed feelings. Most of the players were worrying about their own situations, would they stay or go?

'We went on pre-season tour and new players were arriving all the time, which was funny. One day Wayne Bridge would arrive and someone would leave, the next day Damien Duff turned up, then Geremi, Joe Cole, Veron. He bought a whole new team in a few weeks.'

To add to the surreal nature of that season, Abramovich took to sitting in the dressing room after games, saying nothing, just taking it all in. 'I don't know if he could understand but he would just sit there, like one of the boys,' Gronkjaer said. The season ended with Chelsea second in the Premier League, going out in the semi-finals of the Champions League and the manager Claudio Ranieri getting the sack.

'It was a difficult season. The manager was under pressure straight away as there were rumours about him leaving,' said Gronkjaer. 'He did very well to keep it away from the players and keep the pressure off us.'

Gronkjaer left in the summer of 2004, just before Chelsea started winning trophies under Mourinho, but has no regrets at missing out on the glory years. He moved to Birmingham, then Atletico Madrid and Stuttgart before returning to Denmark and FC Copenhagen.

GOAL 6
Havertz crowns champions of Europe

UEFA Champions League, Final. Chelsea 1-0 Manchester City 0.
Saturday, 29-05-2021 at Estadio do Dragao, Porto.
Attendance 14,110. Havertz (42)

Team: Edouard Mendy, Thiago Silva (Andreas Christensen 39), Toni Rudiger, Cesar Azpilicueta, N'Golo Kante, Jorginho, Reece James, Ben Chilwell, Mason Mount (Mateo Kovacic 80), Kai Havertz, Timo Werner (Christian Pulisic 66).

A CHANT of 'Bring on the Champions, Champions of Europe,' will echo around one of England's great grounds before home games in the 2021-22 season. But it won't be the regular matchday tribute at the Etihad Stadium.

Many expected the Champions League Final to be the day the Sky Blues picked up the ultimate prize to add to their Premier League trophy.

They were wrong. They were out-smarted and out-worked by Thomas Tuchel's team of heroes as Chelsea conquered Europe for the second time in nine years and the vociferous 6,000 fans who'd travelled to the Dragao to support them sounded like 60,000 battle-hardened warriors.

The stars all shone for the team in royal blue. N'Golo Kante was immense in a world class performance as he dominated midfield, consistently stealing the ball from City players.

Mason Mount showed the tenacity and awareness that has seen him rise to such prominence in the last two years. Cesar Azpilicueta, Toni Rudiger and Edouard Mendy were all phenomenal. The whole team worked like a perfectly balanced machine.

German international Kai Havertz chose the perfect stage to show why Chelsea spent £71million on him. He scored the only goal on a beautifully worked break when Mount's pass found him and he rounded Edersen just before half- time.

His moment came in the 42nd minute when Mendy with a precise kick-out found Ben Chilwell who found Mount inside. Mount swivelled and pierced the City defence with a brilliant through ball.

Mount's pass found Havertz and Ederson could only get a light touch on the ball as Havertz knocked it past him and calmly hit his finish left-footed into the empty net.

The travelling army of Chelsea fans - who had endured ticketing problems, Covid restrictions and travel chaos to support their team - roared their approval as the Blues players celebrated the strike.

Tuchel overcame Pep Guardiola for the third time since succeeding Frank Lampard in January - and the City manager cannot escape scrutiny for taking a tactical gamble which backfired.

Guardiola decided against using either Rodri or Fernandinho as a defensive midfielder in favour of an all-out attacking line-up. In truth it left City with a muddled game plan that rarely presented Chelsea with any problems.

Tuchel made it three out of three against Guardiola by producing a disciplined, positive Chelsea performance to the most glorious conclusion.

The German has transformed Chelsea since his arrival making significant changes including restoring Rudiger in central defence and playing the superb man of the match Kante in the midfield-holding position in which he is a world class operator.

The Londoners had the best opportunities throughout, Timo Werner wasting two good chances before Havertz struck and substitute Christian Pulisic squandering another great opportunity in the second half.

Chelsea even survived the first-half loss of experienced defender Thiago Silva to injury, bringing on the excellent Andreas Christensen and carrying on in the same measured, committed fashion.

It was a huge personal victory for Tuchel, who already had wins over

Guardiola in the FA Cup semi-final and in the Premier League at the Etihad Stadium. The confidence and self-belief that those victories bought was in evidence as Chelsea played with a fearless attitude that never allowed City to settle and sparked wild scenes of celebration among players, staff and the fans inside Porto's Estadio do Dragao.

Havertz, the 21-year-old German, had questions asked of him after a sometimes patchy first season in the Premier League.

However, after blossoming in the final he has now written his name into Chelsea's history books after his first-half goal was enough to see the club win our second Champions League title.

Speaking in a television interview immediately following the full-time whistle, a visibly emotional Havertz said, 'I don't know what to say, I really don't know what to say. We deserved it, now we celebrate.

'I waited a long time, I just want to thank my family, my parents, my brother, my sister, my grandmother, my girlfriend. I don't know what to say.'

He was then asked about the pressure of being Chelsea's most expensive outfield player ever, and replied, 'To be honest, right now I don't give a **** about that. We won the ******* Champions League and we're celebrating right now.'

Cesar Azpilicueta joined the interview and said, 'He deserves that, his mentality is top, this guy. He's going to be a superstar, he is already. Not only that, he ran like crazy, that's the team work, that's why he deserves this.'

He also added, 'I came here in 2012 after the Champions League win, I wanted to repeat that. Tonight is amazing, my family are here, it's a special, special day.'

Chelsea captain Azpilicueta went on to lift the trophy as the rest of the team danced joyously around him and they no doubt celebrated long into the night.

The match-winning strike in the final from Havertz was his first Champions League goal. The attacking midfielder was born in Aachen, Germany on June 11, 1999 and became the youngest debutant for

Bayer Leverkusen in the Bundesliga in October, 2016. Chelsea signed Havertz on a five-year contract in September 2020, the transfer fee was reported to be an initial £62 million which could rise to £71 million with add-ons – making him Chelsea's second-most expensive player after Kepa Arrizabalaga.

He made his debut with Chelsea in the Premier League opener, a 3-1 away win against Brighton & Hove Albion. Nine days later he scored his first career hat-trick in a 6-0 home win over Barnsley in the third round of the League Cup.

Havertz scored his first ever Premier League goal in October in a 3-3 draw against Southampton at Stamford Bridge. In November it was revealed that the player had tested positive for Covid-19.

Pundits have described Havertz as a technically gifted, midfielder who is comfortable with the ball on either foot.

During his formative years, his style of play drew early comparisons to compatriot Mesut Ozil with Havertz himself admitting the Arsenal midfielder was a player he looked up to.

By the age of 19 and following numerous impressive performances in the Bundesliga, further comparisons had been drawn between Havertz and former Bayern Leverkusen players such as Michael Ballack and Toni Kroos and some began describing him as a combination of all three an *Alleskonner* – a player who can do everything. Havertz prefers the false nine role which he has been playing at Chelsea.

Following the victory Chelsea boss Tuchel was rewarded with a new contract that will keep him at Stamford Bridge until 2024, as Thiago Silva also agreed a new deal.

The German who led Chelsea to Champions League glory in Porto, signed an initial 18-month deal when he replaced former Champions League winner Lampard as manager.

After the match Tuchel told the club website, 'This is unbelievable. To share it with everybody is unbelievable. I don't know what to feel. I was so grateful to arrive a second time, but I had a feeling this was different. Somehow you could feel it, every day coming closer. The players were determined to win this, we wanted to be the stone in City's shoe.'

Ben Chilwell enjoyed it too, he said 'We knew it would be a tough game. In the second half we fought for our lives to get to this moment, to have this feeling. This is what I came to Chelsea for. It's a dream come true. The key was to get tight and be aggressive. I was getting tired as the game went on but when the Champions League is up for grabs, you don't really tire. It was the best day of my life.'

And Mount added, 'To go all the way in the Champions League, we played some tough teams. At this moment in time, we're the best team in the world. You can't take that away from us.'

Delighted defender Rudiger said, 'It makes me feel proud. This is something I couldn't imagine, but now it's finally true and I will need some days to realise it. Is this real or am I dreaming? It's the greatest day of my career.'

The opposition boss, Guardiola, recognised Chelsea's excellence, 'It was a tight game, we had some almost chances, no clear ones. With the defensive structure of Chelsea it's not easy.'

And some former Blues enjoyed the night, Didier Drogba sent a Tweet that said, 'We believed'. While Fernando Torres wrote, 'Congratulations to Chelsea FC. What a team! Very happy for everyone at the club and especially the all supporters. Very well deserved.' And Michael Ballack Tweeted, 'Absolutely amazing achievement.'

And finally Joe Cole, lifelong fan and ex-player, couldn't contain his joy on the gantry while on punditry duty for television.

Describing Kante's performance as Chelsea won their second Champions League, he said, 'I don't think there is a more important player for his team in world football than N'Golo Kante. He drove this team. I played with Claude Makelele and I thought he was the best in this position until I saw this kid. He is Makelele plus extras.'

GOAL 5
Sublime Osgood heads for cup glory

FA Cup Final replay. Chelsea 2-1 Leeds United.

Wednesday, 29-04-1970 at Old Trafford, Manchester.

Attendance, 62,078. Peter Osgood (78)

Team: Peter Bonetti, Ron Harris, Eddie McCreadie, John Hollins, John Dempsey, David Webb, Tommy Baldwin, Charlie Cooke, Peter Osgood, Ian Hutchinson, Peter Houseman.

The Shed looked up and they saw a great star,
Scoring goals past Pat Jennings from near and from far.
And Chelsea won, as we all knew they would,
And the star of that great team was Peter Osgood.
Osgood, Osgood, Osgood, Osgood.
Born is The King of Stamford Bridge.

CHELSEA in the swinging 'sixties and early 'seventies were the Kings of the King's Road.

But as the cosmopolitan footballers from SW6 became fashion icons and gained film star status there was only one King of Stamford Bridge.

Peter Osgood had scored in every round of the FA Cup and his diving header with 12 minutes to go to equalise in the replay at Old Trafford has become an iconic goal for generations of Chelsea fans.

One young supporter who made the trip to Manchester was the teenaged Neil Barnett who was to go on to have a 32-year working relationship with Chelsea as a writer and pitch announcer.

Known to players and fans alike as the Spy in the Camp, Barnett's first game supporting Chelsea was a 1-0 home victory over Everton in

November, 1959, with Jimmy Greaves scoring the winner.

Back in 1970 to qualify for the Cup Final and replay tickets Spy's family had collected three complete sets of vouchers from Chelsea home programmes. His father drove north for work in advance of the game while he and his mother travelled on the Chelsea special train before standing in the Stretford End.

Spy said, 'Chelsea made it to the replay against all the odds. The Leeds' goalkeeper Gary Sprake hardly touched the ball at Wembley. We managed to stay in the game but Ossie never really got going.

'At Old Trafford he put much more into it. He was a presence throughout the game. At the time Alan Hudson, who manager Dave Sexton had lost to injury, glued the team together. But Ossie led the team.

'We were 1-0 down in the replay when Charlie Cooke dribbled through the middle and delivered a glorious, perfect pass as he saw Ossie making a run. Osgood finished it with a graceful diving header in front of the Chelsea fans.

'Celebrating the goal Ossie put his head down between his hands then clenched his fist as if to say, 'We're back in this now'.

'Everyone who was there sensed from that moment we couldn't be beaten.'

Leeds and Chelsea were two of England's elite teams that season, having finished second and third in the First Division behind Everton.

In a clash of footballing cultures Chelsea were seen as flamboyant, southern softies whereas Leeds were regarded as tough, uncompromising northerners. Neither had won the FA Cup before.

The first match at Wembley finished 2-2 with Chelsea twice coming back from behind. Leeds were generally seen to have had the best of the play with winger Eddie Gray in particular giving David Webb a torrid time.

Jackie Charlton's header after 20 minutes gave the Yorkshiremen the lead but towards the end of the first half a Peter Houseman shot rolled under Gary Sprake's body and drew Chelsea level.

Mick Jones put Leeds ahead six minutes from full-time but two minutes later Ian Hutchinson headed the equaliser from a John Hollins cross. There were no further goals in extra-time and the two teams did a joint lap of honour.

After the game the Wembley pitch was in such terrible state that the FA decided to stage the replay at Manchester United's Old Trafford stadium.

The replay was the only time between 1923 and 2000 that an FA Cup Final was played at a stadium other than Wembley. It attracted a British television audience of more than 28 million, the second highest for a sports broadcast behind the 1966 World Cup Final.

It has been ranked among the greatest ever FA Cup finals and is often named as the 'most brutal' game in the history of English football, due to the undisguised animosity between the two teams.

The referee in charge of both games, Eric Jennings, 47, from Stourbridge, in his last season as a Football League referee, allowed rough play by both sides throughout, playing the advantage rule to its full extent. He booked only one player, Ian Hutchinson of Chelsea.

In 1997 referee David Elleray reviewed the match and concluded that the sides would have received six red cards and twenty yellow cards between them in modern football.

Leeds' manager Don Revie brought in 'keeper David Harvey for Sprake, while Sexton switched Webb for Harris at fullback.

Not long into the game, Chelsea's Harris caught winger Gray with a kick to the back of the knee, an action which hampered the Scotsman for the rest of the match.

Charlton kneed and headbutted Osgood while Chelsea's goalkeeper Peter Bonetti was injured after being bundled into the net by Leeds' Mick Jones, who minutes later, shot past the limping Bonetti for the opening goal.

When Osgood equalised he became the last player to date to have scored in every round of the FA Cup. With the game ending 1–1, the final once again went into extra time.

As the first period of extra time drew to a close Chelsea's Hutchinson sent in a long throw that missed almost every player in the penalty area before being put into the unguarded net by Webb, to give the Blues the lead for the first time in the two games. The FA Cup belonged to Chelsea.

Spy said, 'We were battered at Wembley but the replay was a fantastic day of celebration. Chelsea had a centre forward who loved the spotlight and knew he was top of the bill. We won the League in 1955, now we had the Cup in 1970.'

In the following season Chelsea reached the final of the European Cup Winners Cup, played in Piraeus, Greece, at Karaiskakis Stadium where they faced Real Madrid.

After yet another final that went into a replay, the first game a 1–1 draw with a goal from Osgood and the second giving Chelsea a 2-1 victory with goals from Dempsey and Osgood earning the Blues their first European trophy.

When The King of Stamford Bridge sadly died in March 2006, his wife Lynne set up The Peter Osgood Trust to help under-privileged children get involved in football.

At the Trust's inaugural event proceedings started with a rendition of The King of Stamford Bridge chant heard so often from the terraces and stands at The Bridge.

Lynne said, 'It's great to see so many fans and former players here. Chelsea was Ossie's club. He loved every minute of his time here and he loved the fans. Once The King, always The King, I say - and Ossie is The King of Stamford Bridge.'

The late Tommy Docherty, who was manager at The Bridge from 1962-67, said, 'Ossie was the best player I have ever seen. He had the grace to glide past players with ease and nothing ever troubled him. He played football with a smile on his face and loved life. He was a true gentleman and it was a pleasure to be his coach.'

Former teammate Bobby Tambling has talked about Osgood at length, 'There was simply nobody like him,' he said. 'A lot of the Chelsea players in that team had come through together from a young age and had to work their way up through the ranks, but Ossie was different.

'At 17 he was in the first-team because he was that good. The first time the players saw him train we all knew he was going to be a great player for Chelsea and he never let us down. He was excellent.'

Clive Walker, who was at the club when Ossie made his emotional return after four years at Southampton, said, 'I had grown up watching him from The Shed and then to suddenly be playing alongside him was incredible. He was a legend at Chelsea.'

Former captain, leader, legend John Terry declared, 'Ossie, we love you. Long live the King.'

Frank Lampard said, 'I have so much respect for Ossie. He is a Chelsea legend – a big hero of mine.'

Lampard went on to add an insight into his goal celebration when he kissed the penalty spot after scoring against Derby some months after Osgood's ashes were buried under the spot in October 2006.

'I had been desperate to score there since his ashes were buried. I went to the ceremony and it was a very emotional occasion. I'd been waiting for a penalty there for so long and it was just a mark of respect for a Chelsea hero.'

Finally, my personal memory of Ossie was shaking his hand in Stockholm before the Cup Winners Cup Final against Stuttgart as he sat laughing and joking among the Chelsea fans.

GOAL 4
Chelsea are back for Highbury hello

League Division One. Arsenal 1-1 Chelsea.

Saturday, 25-08-84 at Highbury.

Attendance, 45,329. Kerry Dixon (39).

Team: Eddie Niedzwiecki, Colin Lee, Doug Rougvie, Colin Pates, Joe McLaughlin, Dale Jasper, Pat Nevin, Nigel Spackman, Kerry Dixon, David Speedie, Paul Canoville.

MY brother and I had planned an early start for Chelsea's first game back in the First Division, an 11.30am kick-off against Arsenal at Highbury.

He had to travel from Coventry where he was working whereas I only had to take the Underground from Ealing Broadway.

I was due to meet him at Leicester Square station on the northbound Piccadilly line platform at 9.30am so we could beat the crowds. This wasn't a good plan.

Ealing Broadway, at the end of the District line was busy for a Saturday morning, perhaps 50 Chelsea fans boarded the train then most changed at Acton Town for the Piccadilly line train on the opposite platform which was standing room only. As the train rattled through West London more supporters squeezed in at Hammersmith, Barons Court and Earl's Court.

The station announcer at Earl's Court was saying the next Piccadilly Line train is just two minutes behind, 'Do not try to board this train.' By the time we were approaching Leicester Square I had edged my way to the doors.

The whole train was rocking in a rendition of 'Carefree wherever you may be', but as we rolled into the station this was completely overwhelmed by an immense swell of noise, 'Hello, hello. Chelsea are back, Chelsea are back.'

Every square inch available was occupied by Chelsea, youngsters were on their dad's shoulders, people were standing on the wooden benches and crushed into alcoves and entrance ways; how they let so many people on to the platform baffles me to this day.

I somehow managed to get out and let the sea of new faces flow around me. Very few made it on to the train, then the doors wouldn't close, twice. Finally the driver edged away and the next train was due in one minute. I found my petrified brother plastered all over an advert for a London show.

So began our day of tunnels, Chelsea, beer and sunshine. We arrived at the cavernous Arsenal Underground station which echoed with noise as we moved slowly back up to daylight, only to get in line behind thousands of Chelsea fans waiting for tickets.

By 10.30am we were inside and, by 11am the old terrace was resonating to the chants of the tens of thousands of Chelsea fans that made the game feel like a home derby at The Bridge.

The Clock End was bursting at the seams the temperature was rising, a sea of limbs; clapping, cheering, singing. Chels giving our team the best away support ever. There were Chelsea in every stand awaiting our team, roaring them back to where we all knew they belonged.

Away trips to Rotherham, Barnsley, Scarborough and Crewe were history now, 'We are the famous, the famous Chelsea.' The match is all a bit of a blur to many of us, but everyone who attended will never forget our day in the sunshine at the Highbury Library.

Kerry Dixon remembers the fixture well, 'Pre-season training on the sand dunes of Aberystwyth had got me fit and I was feeling excited about my debut in the First Division.

'Chelsea were back in the top flight after seven years, playing London rivals Arsenal on a hot, sunny morning. We received a massive welcome from our supporters at Highbury; there must have been over 20,000

Blues fans in the ground and the Clock End was packed.'

'It was incredible really, the sheer number of Chelsea fans packed into the Clock End. We knew the support was going to be something special when the team bus took ten minutes from the top of the hill to the main entrance at the ground. There were Chelsea fans everywhere.'

As usual at Highbury a marching band was on the pitch to entertain the crowd with 'Guantanamera' and 'When The Saints Go Marching In', but they were completely drowned out by the noise coming from Chelsea's fans.

Half an hour before kick-off as the teams ran out for a warm-up the packed ground reverberated to 'Chelsea are back'. At this stage the sheer magnitude of the away support was evident and the Arsenal fans were strangely quiet.

Chelsea were without Welshmen Joey Jones who was suspended, and Mickey Thomas and John Bumstead through injuries. Paul Canoville and Dale Jasper deputised. As the tension continued to build every Chelsea player had his name chanted individually and each acknowledged the tribute.

Arsenal striker Tony Woodcock managed a smile during warm-up; after his recent drink-driving problems the Chelsea hordes in the Clock End serenaded him with, 'You've come all this way, on the bus.'

After going back to the dressing room for some last-minute instructions the teams finally emerged into the sweltering cauldron of heat and noise. The tightly packed Clock End only made the heat more uncomfortable.

Jasper could have given the visitors the lead when his shot from outside the box was pushed away by Arsenal 'keeper Pat Jennings. The atmosphere was electric. Eddie Niedzwiecki made a series of great saves to keep the score 0-0.

After 35 minutes Arsenal finally took the lead when Pat Nevin gave away a free-kick. Paul Mariner scored a header in front of the North Bank from captain Kenny Sansom's cross. However, four minutes later Dixon had his chance.

Chelsea were given a free-kick of their own. Doug Rougvie's long ball forward was met by Dixon whose left-footed shot was parried by Jennings. The ball came back to the striker whose right-footed volley scorched into the back of the net.

The massed ranks of Blue erupted to salute their side's first goal of the season. But somehow it was more than that, much more. After the years of hurt Chelsea really were back. The goal, the photo of Dixon's triumphant leap and the image of Chelsea fans' ecstatic celebration in the Clock End have become iconic records of the day.

The second half of the game was all a bit of a blur. There were good chances at both ends but a draw seemed a fair result. New signing Rougvie began to earn cult status with the Chelsea fans as England's Viv Anderson slightly overran the ball; Rougvie went into the tackle so hard that Anderson went into orbit, much to the delight of the Chelsea supporters.

Rougvie was awestruck by the passion of the Blues' followers, after the match he said, 'I've seen many Celtic-Rangers contests but what happened today outshone even those occasions.'

When the referee blew for fulltime the Chelsea hordes were in full voice again. The reception afforded to the players said it all as 'Chelsea are back' turned into a thunderous rendition of 'We're proud of you Chelsea'.

It was a great result for Chelsea, a defeat would have been a such an anti-climax for everyone involved. Dixon had scored his goal and the campaign was underway.

Dixon said, 'It's been well documented this was my favourite goal for Chelsea, but let me explain. It wasn't just the goal it was the whole package, the day itself that encapsulated my thoughts and gives me a feeling of nostalgia.

'It was the sheer number of Chelsea supporters in every stand, it was the sunshine, it was the way we played. We were back in the First Division and proved we could compete with an Arsenal side with an international defence.

'I scored a volley against the great Pat Jennings. Chelsea had only recently been promoted but we earned a 1-1 draw at Highbury.'

During his later years with the Blues there were times when Dixon struggled but when he had the goal in his sight he was instantly transformed.

He was signed from Reading in August 1983 by Neal as part of his extensive rebuilding programme and began to repay the £175,000 fee at once with two goals on the opening day of the season in a 5-0 victory at home to Derby.

The striker was fortunate that the players around complemented his style so well. He was superb in the air and thrived on an endless series of inch-perfect crosses from Nevin on the right, like the one at Grimsby that clinched promotion back to the First Division.

Dixon said, 'Again the travelling Chelsea support was phenomenal. Our fans were packed in behind the fencing like sardines and there were pockets of our supporters all around the ground.

'We won the game 1-0, won the Second Division title and went back to the team hotel as guests at a wedding reception being held that evening!'

As he built his career at Chelsea Dixon's best asset was his blistering pace and he quickly established a partnership with David Speedie. The gritty Yorkshireman making sure Dixon was supplied with plenty of through balls.

Dixon earned his first international caps during England's 1985 summer tour of North America and he was included in the squad for the 1986 World Cup.

The next two seasons proved frustrating and a transfer seemed likely but Dixon stayed at Stamford Bridge scoring 25 goals in another Second Division Championship victory in 1988/89.

On Chelsea's return to the First Division under Bobby Campbell, Dixon scored regularly but as his pace faded and the supply of passes dried up, a move was on the cards. In July 1992 he was sold to Southampton for £575,000. He scored 193 goals for Chelsea, just short of Bobby Tambling's (and now Frank Lampard's) record.

On Saturday, April 4, 1994, Dixon nearing the end of his career, played for Luton in a FA Cup semi-final against Chelsea at Wembley. Chelsea's 2-0 win, with both goals from Gavin Peacock, couldn't spoil the day for Dixon as time after time nearly 60,000 fans roared out, 'There's only one Kerry Dixon, one Kerry Dixon.'

'It was the most humbling moment in my footballing life,' said Dixon. 'I was playing for my home town club against the club I love. The noise was incredible, absolutely unbelievable.'

And finally, back to *that* day at Highbury and as the much-loved, television football commentator, the late Brian Moore, said, 'Kerry Dixon with 34 goals last season gets away to the best possible start in the First Division.'

GOAL 3
Super Frank fires Blues to title ecstasy

Premier League. Bolton Wanderers 0-2 Chelsea.
Saturday, 30-04-2005. Reebok Stadium.
Attendance, 27,653. Frank Lampard (60, 76)

Team: Petr Cech, Geremi, Ricardo Carvalho, John Terry, William Gallas, Tiago, Claude Makelele (Alexey Smertin 89), Frank Lampard, Jiri Jarosik, Didier Drogba (Robert Huth 65), Gudjohnsen (Joe Cole 85).

BEFORE the 2004-05 campaign started the Special One predicted Chelsea would win the title in the away fixture at Bolton Wanderers.

Manager Jose Mourinho was asking a lot of his players in a team that hadn't been champions since captain Roy Bentley lifted the trophy half a century earlier.

In 1954 food rationing following the Second World War had only just ended, beer was 1s 4d (6.5p) a pint and a black and white television was considered a luxury item.

But on April 30 at the Reebok Stadium, Frank Lampard struck twice in the second half as Mourinho added the Premiership to the Carling Cup in his first season in charge.

Chelsea had beaten West London neighbours Fulham 3-1 on April 23 and could have been gifted the title on the Monday if Arsenal had failed to beat Tottenham Hotspur at Highbury.

However, Arsenal won the game 1-0 and the potential title decider moved on to Chelsea's game at Bolton.

John Terry said, 'I didn't really want the chase to end like that. I wanted to win it on the pitch and celebrate on the pitch.'

The Blues did not field the under-strength side that had been expected although Joe Cole was on the bench and Damien Duff and Arjen Robben both missed the game through injury.

Chelsea had only won once in their six previous visits to Bolton and they were fully tested in a torrid first 45 minutes in which they were subjected to an aerial barrage.

Stellios Giannakopoulos tested Cech early on, while Gary Speed also forced the big Czech 'keeper into a fine save with a header.

The Blues were limited as an attacking force in the first-half and they were grateful when Kevin Davies headed straight into the arms of Cech from just six yards when he was found unmarked from Bruno N'Gotty's free-kick.

On the stroke of half-time there was concern for Terry who had been caught in the eye by the flailing arm of Davies. Terry was on the ground for several minutes before returning to the action, although there was word from the dressing room that he was suffering from impaired vision.

However, it would take more than a knock to stop Terry. Likewise, Mourinho had gone for substance over style in his team selection. He had started with Geremi at right-back and Jiri Jarosik in midfield to give the team more height and muscle to cope with Bolton's tactics.

Mourinho had torn into the team at half-time and his rant worked as Chelsea looked a more formidable unit after the interval.

He wanted his players to show more mettle and Jarosik did just that as he won an aerial duel to give Didier Drogba the chance to flick on for Lampard.

Nothing seemed to be on as Lampard was ushered away from goal just inside the area and in the direction of the corner flag, harassed by Vincent Candela.

He eventually shrugged him off and cut back inside, keeping calm he sent Jussi Jaaskelainen the wrong way with a powerful shot to put the Blues ahead, in front of 3,000 rapturous Chelsea fans behind the goal.

Drogba had been involved in running verbal battles with Bolton's defence and it was no surprise when he was replaced by defender Robert Huth five minutes after Lampard's goal.

Bolton then began an aerial bombardment of Chelsea's goal, pulling nearly every man forward. Speed's long throw was unwittingly deflected towards his own goal by Geremi, but Cech somehow dived to his right to turn the ball to safety.

And the goalkeeper's worth to Chelsea was underlined as they sprang forward to put their name on the title with 15 minutes left.

Bolton were caught hopelessly up-field as Lampard broke forward and rounded Jaaskelainen to score and send Chelsea's army of fans into ecstasy.

After the game Lampard said, 'We've proved that the best team wins the League. There have been some harsh words spoken about us not being entertaining and that the best two teams in the Premier League are in the final of the FA Cup (Manchester United and Arsenal). But the best team wins the League and we have done that.

'You look at Arsenal, who lost at Bolton, and Manchester United who drew, but we went up there and won. It's time for others to take a look and know that we are definitely the best.'

Exactly three years later it was an emotional night for Lampard who was back in the Chelsea starting line-up for the first time since the death of his mother, Pat. She had passed away after a battle with pneumonia and her death had brought a cloud of sorrow over Stamford Bridge.

Chelsea made two changes to the teams that started the first-leg of the UEFA Champions League semi-final at Anfield, Michael Essien returning from a European ban and Saloman Kalou preferred to Florent Malouda.

It had been a John Arne Riise own goal in the 90th minute at Anfield that had put Chelsea in control of the tie. Dirk Kuyt had put Liverpool ahead in the first half, but Riise would head in a Kalou cross to give Chelsea a precious away goal.

Didier Drogba opened the scoring with a 12-yard strike but a Fernando Torres drive sent the game into extra-time.

The extra period fizzled with controversy, sparked when an Essien drive from 22 yards out flew into the net, only to be ruled out because four Chelsea players stood offside. The Blues protests that they were not interfering with play were muted seconds later, though, as Sami Hyypia felled Ballack to give Chelsea a penalty.

Lampard looked calm and composed as he slotted home the penalty but as he celebrated by kissing a black armband worn in remembrance of his mother and pointed to the rain-lashed sky above, the emotions flooded out.

Seven minutes later Chelsea put the game out of Liverpool's reach when Drogba swept home Nicolas Anelka's pass from six yards. Ryan Babel reduced the arrears just before full-time.

Chelsea's win was sweet revenge, having been knocked out at the semi-final stage three times in the previous four years, including twice by Liverpool in 2005 and 2007.

And it was fully deserved on a tumultuous night's football, their reward being a Champions League Final clash with Premier League rivals Manchester United.

A number of years later Lampard said, 'I always dedicate my goals to my mum. I lost her a couple of years ago. She was my biggest supporter and is always with me.'

Fast-forward to Villa Park on May 11, 2013. Lampard struck his 202nd and 203rd goals in a Chelsea shirt to pass Bobby Tambling's all-time goalscoring record for the club.

With Chelsea trailing to Christian Benteke's first-half strike, the 34-year-old coolly collected a pass from Eden Hazard, switched the ball to his left foot and fired pass Ben Guzan from 15 yards.

His second came after clever play on the left from Ashley Cole and Hazard, before the latter squared for Lampard to slot home from close range.

Bobby Tambling, who scored 202 goals for the Blues between 1959 and 1970, held the record for 47 years and was clearly emotional as he was brought out onto the Stamford Bridge pitch for half-time of Chelsea's 2-0 win over Swansea.

The former striker has been unwell and was admitted to hospital for three months and Lampard was the first to mention his predecessor after the Villa game.

He said, 'Bobby Tambling is a great man, he hasn't been well lately but he's a great man.

'I was pleased to level it but I didn't want to overcook that celebration out of respect for him. But to then go and break it, I was delighted.'

Tambling paid tribute to the England midfielder, saying he was pleased to be losing the title to Lampard, who he called Chelsea's 'greatest ever player'.

'If you take what Frank has done personally and then add in what Chelsea have done as a team in the last 10 years, he must surely go down not just as one of the greats but probably the greatest Chelsea player ever. He thinks like a striker, performs like a striker.'

'We all thought Kerry Dixon was going to do it but I believed from four or five years ago that Frank would be the one.'

Lampard was born in Romford, London and attended Brentwood School, achieving 11 GCSEs. He was signed by Chelsea from West Ham for £11million in 2001. The box-to-box midfielder enjoyed a hugely successful 13-year playing career with the Blues winning multiple trophies before returning for a spell as manager in 2019.

Player, goalscoring record holder and manager, Super Frankie Lampard said, 'This club becomes you. Once you've played for it, you're always welcomed back for the rest of your life, so you become Chelsea and it becomes you.'

GOAL 2
Walker's winner signals great escape

Second Division. Bolton Wanderers 0-1 Chelsea.
Saturday, 07-05-83 at Burnden Park.
Attendance 8,687. Clive Walker (70)

Team, Steve Francis, Joey Jones, Chris Hutchings, Gary Chivers, Micky Droy, Colin Pates, Mike Fillery, John Bumstead, Colin Lee, Paul Canoville, Clive Walker.

EUROPEAN glory was a million miles away at rain-soaked Burnden Park when Clive Walker scored perhaps the most significant goal in Chelsea's history.

In the '82-83 season any hope of challenging for a promotion place had soon disappeared and it became clear the campaign could end with the Blues finishing in their lowest ever League position.

In January when the team embarked on a disastrous run of just three wins in 20 games the threat of relegation loomed large.

Chelsea travelled to Bolton Wanderers for the penultimate game of the season knowing that realistically only a win would save the club from the third division and almost inevitable financial meltdown.

Bolton were one of 11 clubs that could still go down and the scene was set for a tense affair. The flow of the game was not helped by the appalling weather conditions. For much of the match it looked as if neither team would score, and then with 20 minutes remaining Clive Walker netted the crucial goal from outside the area.

When the final whistle finally sounded the 3,500 Chelsea fans, who made-up almost half of the attendance and were now thoroughly soaked, danced in delight and relief.

The win was followed by a goalless draw with Middlesbrough in our final game at The Bridge, but it was only when news came through of other results that we were finally safe.

Looking back to the crucial Bolton fixture, Walker said, 'The team that day was 100 per cent focused on not getting relegated. We had been on a terrible run in the League and knew it was now or never.'

Most of the team played cards on the coach on the way up North, a culture in '80s football that Walker enjoyed and helped him relax. Manager John Neal's team talk was low-key but giant defender Micky Droy had the players ready for battle.

Walker said, 'When we ran out on to the pitch and looked over to our left there were thousands of Chelsea fans closely penned in on the uncovered away terrace.

'The travelling support was fabulous, the number of fans who made the trip was unbelievable. It gave all the players a real buzz.

'The game itself was a poor affair with few chances and looked like it might end with a point apiece.

'The rain was relentless and players were making mistakes as they slipped in the mud. After about 70 minutes I found some space and ran onto the ball about 25 yards out and decided to shoot.'

The rest is history. Walker's drive beat Bolton 'keeper Jim McDonagh and Chelsea were spared the ignominy of Third Division football or financial disintegration.

'At the end of the game some of the players including myself and Chris Hutchings went over to the travelling support to throw them our shirts. They had been brilliant and it was our way of saying thank you,' said Walker.

Walker's ability to redeem a hopeless cause had been seen before against Bolton in October 1978. With 20 minutes remaining he came on as a substitute at Stamford Bridge with Chelsea trailing 0-3 to the Wanderers.

The 21-year-old's electrifying pace inspired comeback goals from Kenny Swain, Tommy Langley and Walker himself before the unfortunate Sam Allardyce sliced into his own net to give Chelsea an unlikely 4-3 victory.

However, Walker's biggest contribution to Chelsea folklore had come earlier that season in the FA Cup 3rd round against Liverpool at Stamford Bridge.

At the end of the '74-75 season Chelsea had been relegated to the Second Division but bounced back and after a couple of seasons were once again in the top flight.

Things didn't look good for the Blues progression in the competition when they were drawn to play Liverpool, champions of England, champions of Europe and recent UEFA Super Cup winners beating Hamburg 7-1 on aggregate.

Since Chelsea's 1970 FA Cup victory the team had not made it any further than the quarter-finals.

Nevertheless, a crowd of 45,449 packed into The Bridge to see Chelsea without captain Ray Wilkins or defender Micky Droy take on the champions.

Walker had scored in the two previous games, a 4-5 win at Birmingham City and a 2-2 draw with West Bromwich Albion at The Bridge.

'It was a fantastic day,' said Walker, 'The size of the crowd, the huge noise even the presence of the Liverpool fans added to the atmosphere. It was a big occasion.'

'Bob Paisley had switched Phil Neal to left-back with Joey Jones to right-back, I thought maybe with the idea Joey was going to give me a lively time.

'From a throw in after about 16 minutes I slipped past Joey, kept my head down and let fly a left foot shot from outside the box.

'Sometimes when you strike a football you know you've hit the sweet spot, it happens from time to time. The shot had swerve and pace and I knew it was going past Ray Clemence as soon as I struck the ball.'

'The swell of noise from the around the ground was immense and The Shed went crazy. We were used to playing in front of perhaps

10,000 spectators but there were over 45,000 there on the day. It was my once in a lifetime goal.'

The home support seemed confident of a win but there was still 75 minutes to play. Chelsea made it to half-time at 1-0 losing Charlie Cooke with a pulled muscle but replacing him with Steve Finnieston.

Ken Shellito's young side had done well and unbelievably within ten minutes of the re-start they had taken a 3-0 lead. Finnieston hit a low shot into the bottom right-hand corner of the net to make it 2-0, then Tommy Langley latched on to a short backpass from Phil Neal to chip the ball over the advancing Clemence.

Liverpool's Dave Johnson scored to make it 3-1 before Walker was in action again. Bill Garner controlled a long cross on his chest before playing it short in the penalty area to Walker who hit the ball home.

The pressure was suddenly off and Walker remembers celebrating in front of the roaring, swaying Shed End. 'The Chelsea fans were brilliant that day, absolutely exceptional. I wanted to share the moment with them and my teammates.

Kenny Dalglish scored a headed consolation goal past Peter Bonetti in a crowded Chelsea penalty area near the end, but it wasn't enough to stop the Blues.

'We did well with eight or nine players who had come up from the youth ranks. We had a good game and beat the champions of England and Europe convincingly,' said Walker.

Liverpool manager Bob Paisley described his team's performance as 'pathetic' and the feeblest he had seen since the team's relegation to the Second Division 24 years earlier.

Chelsea thrashed Burnley 6-2 in the Fourth Round of the cup, but lost 1-2 in the fifth round replay at The Bridge to Leyton Orient of Division Two.

Walker was a schoolboy with Chelsea at the age of 14, an apprentice at 16 and a professional at 17. He scored 65 goals for Chelsea in 191 games. He played the first eight games of the '83-84 promotion season under John Neal scoring four goals before sustaining a broken jaw in a goalless draw against Middlesbrough. He was out for six weeks and was never able to re-establish himself in the team after the emergence of Pat Nevin and Paul Canoville. At the end of the season, slightly disillusioned, he decided it was time to move on.

After signing for Sunderland he received a warm reception from fans at Stamford Bridge in the second game of the season which Chelsea won 1-0 with a Canoville goal.

Later that season the reception wasn't quite so cordial when Chelsea played the second-leg of the Football League Cup semi-final at Stamford Bridge. The Blues were trailing 2-0 from the first-leg played with a weakened team in atrocious icy conditions at Roker Park.

In the 2-3 home defeat by Sunderland, Walker scored twice and was hit in the back of the head by an irate fan who had run onto the pitch.

Walker was a Chelsea player for 13 years and clearly has an affinity with the club. He said, 'I am, and always will be, a Chelsea fan. My two grown up sons also follow the Blues.

'I have had two wonderful careers, 26 years as a footballer and now 20 years working in the football media.

'I've played for some great clubs with some great teammates. I even had a spell on loan from Chelsea one summer at Fort Lauderdale Strikers where I played with George Best and Gerd Muller.'

GOAL 1
Drogba the destroyer on day of destiny

European Champions League Final. Bayern Munich 1-1 Chelsea.
(Chelsea win 4-3 on penalties)
Saturday,19-05-2012 at the Allianz Arena, Munich.
Attendance, 69,901. Didier Drogba (88 + fifth penalty)

Team: Team, Petr Cech, Jose Bosingwa, David Luiz, Gary Cahill, Ashley Cole, Salomon Kalou (Fernando Torres 84), Jon Obi Mikel, Frank Lampard, Ryan Bertrand (Florent Malouda 73), Juan Mata, Didier Drogba.

BAYERN Munich were the overwhelming favourites. The Champions League Final was in their stadium, the awesome Allianz Arena. They had their own supporters, in their city, in their country.

In 2011-12 They were runners up in the Bundesliga and the German Cup but had been the country's strongest team in the previous decade.

They had Manuel Neuer, Franck Ribery, Bastian Schweinsteiger, Mario Gomez, Thomas Muller, Philipp Lahm, Jerome Boateng, Toni Kroos and former Blue, Arjen Robben.

They strode out onto the pitch with pride, perhaps even a little arrogance, focused on the task ahead. They had one match to take the European Champions League crown. To show their footballing superiority. To prove they were the indisputably the best club side in Europe.

But they weren't Chelsea. They didn't know about glorious unpredictability. And they didn't have Didier Drogba.

When Roberto Di Matteo took the reins at Chelsea after the departure of Andre Villas Boas, winning the title was an impossible dream but the

Blues were still fighting in two cup competitions.

In the FA Cup fifth round replay at Birmingham City's St. Andrews ground, second half goals from Juan Mata and Raul Meireles put us through to a quarter-final clash with Leicester City and a 5-2 victory. Spurs were the semi-final opponents at Wembley when the Blues achieved a memorable 5-1 success.

In the FA Cup Final at Wembley Chelsea dominated against Liverpool and goals from Ramires and Didier Drogba were enough for the Blues to lift the trophy despite a late consolation strike from Andy Carroll.

Di Matteo continued his personal story of Wembley triumph leading Chelsea to the 2012 FA Cup win. Previously, in 1997 he had scored after 43 seconds in the 2-0 FA Cup final victory over Middlesbrough and the following year was on target again against Boro in the 2-0 League Cup final win. He also scored the only goal of the game in the last FA Cup final at the old Wembley, a 1-0 success against Aston Villa.

Two weeks after the Cup success against Liverpool, Di Matteo's team walked onto the pitch to face Bayern Munich at the Allianz Arena. The team had to put the Champions League heartache of 2008 in Moscow against Manchester United behind them.

The pressure was immense because Chelsea had finished sixth in the Premier League and would not qualify for the following season's Champions League unless they could win the competition and enter as champions.

Chelsea were without four key players, John Terry, Branislav Ivanovic, Ramires and Raul Meireles, meanwhile Gary Cahill and David Luiz hadn't played for a month.

When Portuguese referee Pedro Proenca blew his whistle to start the game captain Frank Lampard and every Chelsea player on the pitch knew what had to be done.

In the first-half the Blues support was in good voice as the huge Pride of London flag was displayed. Chelsea had quickly sold their 17,500 allocation of tickets and many thousands more had been acquired by fans by other means.

Chelsea were attacking the German supporters in the first-half, Ashley Cole went in hard on Toni Kroos to give away a free-kick in the opening moments.

Chelsea's first attack came with six minutes played, some clever passing leading to an overhit Drogba cross.

Bayern were dominating possession without looking like they could threaten the well organised Chelsea defence, then on 35 minutes Thomas Muller was found unmarked near the penalty spot but volleyed wide.

Suddenly at the other end Ryan Bertrand found Drogba who played the ball wide to Salomon Kalou, his low and hard shot forced the first save out of Manuel Neuer.

However, just before half-time as Chelsea pressed Bayern became more of a counter-attacking force and Gomez shot over when presented with a great chance.

First-half statistics showed Bayern with 60 per cent of possession and 13 attempts on goal to just two from Chelsea. The second half started with some important blocks and defensive tackles especially from David Luiz and Cole as the Bayern attack moved up a notch.

Drogba tried a spectacular effort on goal on the turn but didn't trouble Neuer.

Bayern continued to drag shots wide and Chelsea's attacking potential from Mata was crowded out time and time again.

After 82 minutes Kroos was able to cross unchallenged towards the far post and Muller headed down, beating Cech with a ball that bounced up over the Chelsea 'keeper.

With just eight minutes remaining and Fernando Torres on for Kalou it seemed that time was running out for the Blues.

However, you should never underestimate the man from the Ivory Coast in a cup final. Mata put a corner over towards the near post and Drogba thundered a header past Neuer and under the bar. The noise from the Chelsea fans gathered behind the goal was apocalyptic. The roar of lions.

With three minutes of extra-time played Drogba caught the heel of Ribery to give away a penalty. It was Robben against his friend big Petr Cech. The pressure told and Cech saved low down to his left. Maybe, just maybe.

Ribery was replaced by Ivica Olic following the foul by Drogba. Despite a couple of goalmouth scrambles and some bookings extra-time ended scoreless.

In the penalty shoot-out at the Bayern end of the stadium Cech got his hand to the first penalty from Lahm but couldn't keep it out. Neuer then saved from Mata.

Gomez made it 2-0 to Bayern but Luiz scored powerfully with his penalty to make it 2-1.

Neuer the Bayern 'keeper beat Cech making it 3-1 before Lampard made it 3-2.

Substitute Olic stepped up to take Bayern's fourth penalty but had it saved by the outstretched arm of Cech and Cole drew the scores level at 3-3.

Bastian Schweinsteiger was next on the spot but Cech got his fingers to the shot and it hit the post. Drogba had his chance and the Ivorian hit the ball to his left as Neuer dived the other way, 4-3. Chelsea were champions of Europe for the first time.

As breaking waves of joy crashed through the almost unbelieving Chelsea ranks the vast travelling army saluted their heroes. Carefree.

Neil Barnett, Chelsea's spy in the camp, said, 'The equaliser was the absolute epitome of the man. It was Didier what did you expect?'

'He was a brilliant, brilliant, big game player. The best centre forward we've ever had. The best in the world.'

Spy returned to the team hotel and joined the celebrations, 'I didn't go to bed and on the coach to take the plane home the next morning I couldn't speak until the adrenaline kicked in.'

Drogba said, 'It was fate. I believe a lot in destiny. It was written a long time ago but we did not know.

'This team is amazing and I want to dedicate this cup to all the managers we've had before, the players I've played with before. It's fantastic. The lesson is always believe.'

And Cahill, who played late on in the match while struggling with cramp, said, 'We have a group of players that have a big heart, passion, motivation and desire. That was the only way to be able to and it's been an immense effort by the whole group.

'Didier has been incredible for this club. He scored a fantastic goal to keep us in the game and then the winning penalty. It's been incredible.'

Television pundit Jamie Carragher was also generous with his praise for the Ivorian, 'Drogba did what all great strikers do and that is score in the biggest games. He scored three winners in FA Cup finals, got the crucial goals in two League Cup finals and who could forget what he did in Munich. At his best he was unplayable.'

Gary Neville said, 'They're crying. It was Drogba. It was the angels, it was the heavens, it was the stars, it was the gods, it was everything for Chelsea.

'This is not anything to do with football, this is spirit. Never giving up, fighting to the end, that English spirit running right through this Champions League for Chelsea.'

Jose Mourinho added, 'He was a great player, a great friend and somebody who will be part of my life forever. Drogba is a fighter. He is the kind of player I would say - with you I could go to war.'

Sky Sports' Martin Tyler, commentating on the game exclaimed, 'Drogbaaa!!! And he's pulled the rabbit out of the hat again! Can you believe it? Chelsea just won't let go of the Champions League.'

And finally, captain Frank Lampard said, 'I think it was meant to be. We keep bouncing back. We never wanted to say it too much but this is the one we really wanted.'

BIBLIOGRAPHY

100 years of the Blues 1905-2006 - Ron Hockings
©The Hockings family 2007

Stamford Bridge Legends - David Lane
Legends Publishing 2003

Kings of Europe - Chelsea FC
Trinity Mirror Sport Media 2012

Champions 2014-15 Chelsea FC
Trinity Mirror Sport Media 2015

Champions 2016-17 - Chelsea FC
Trinity Mirror Sport Media 2017

John Terry 50 Defining Fixtures - Garry Hayes
Amberley Publishing 2016

Up Front - Kerry Dixon
John Blake Publishing 2016

Black and Blue - Paul Canoville and Rick Glanvill
Headline Publishing Group 2008

Perfect 10 - Neil Barnett
Trinity Mirror Sport Media 2008

Celery! Representing Chelsea in '80s - Kelvin Barker
DPS Publishing 2006

100 Memorable Matches - Chelsea Chadder
Gate 17 2018

Chelsea Player by Player - Peter Lovering
Guinness Publishing 1993

ONLINE

bbc.co.uk/sport/football

skysports.com/football

thetimes.co.uk/sport/football

dailymail.co.uk/sport/football

dailystar.co.uk/sport/football

mirror.co.uk/sport/football

thesun.co.uk/sport/football

metro.co.uk/sport/football

theguardian.com/football

standard.co.uk/sport/football

telegraph.co.uk/football

en.wikipedia.org

GATE 17
THE COMPLETE COLLECTION
(AUTUMN 2021)

CHELSEA

Over Land and Sea – Mark Worrall
Chelsea here, Chelsea There – Kelvin Barker, David Johnstone, Mark Worrall
Chelsea Football Fanzine – the best of cfcuk
One Man Went to Mow – Mark Worrall
Chelsea Chronicles (Five Volume Series) – Mark Worrall
Making History Not Reliving It –
Kelvin Barker, David Johnstone, Mark Worrall
Celery! Representing Chelsea in the 1980s – Kelvin Barker
Stuck On You, a year in the life of a Chelsea supporter – Walter Otton
Palpable Discord, a year of drama and dissent at Chelsea – Clayton Beerman
Rhyme and Treason – Carol Ann Wood
Eddie Mac Eddie Mac – Eddie McCreadie's Blue & White Army
The Italian Job, A Chelsea thriller starring Antonio Conte – Mark Worrall
Carefree! Chelsea Chants & Terrace Culture – Mark Worrall, Walter Otton
Diamonds, Dynamos and Devils – Tim Rolls
Arrivederci Antonio, The Italian Job (part two) – Mark Worrall
Where Were You When We Were Shocking? – Neil L. Smith
Chelsea, 100 Memorable Games – Chelsea Chadder
Bewitched, Bothered & Bewildered – Carol Ann Wood
Stamford Bridge Is Falling Down – Tim Rolls
Cult Fiction – Dean Mears
Chelsea, If Twitter Was Around When… – Chelsea Chadder
Blue Army – Vince Cooper
Liquidator 1969-70 A Chelsea Memoir – Mark Worrall
When Skies Are Grey, Super Frank, Chelsea And The Coronavirus Crisis – Mark Worrall
Tales Of The (Chelsea) Unexpected – David Johnstone & Neil L Smith
The Ultimate Unofficial Chelsea Quiz Book – Chelsea Chadder
Blue Days – Chris Wright
Let The Celery Decide – Walter Otton
Blue Hitmen – Paul Radcliffe
Sexton For God – Tim Rolls

FICTION

Blue Murder, Chelsea Till I Die – Mark Worrall
The Wrong Outfit – Al Gregg
The Red Hand Gang – Walter Otton
Coming Clean – Christopher Morgan
This Damnation – Mark Worrall
Poppy – Walter Otton

NON FICTION

Roe2Ro – Walter Otton
Shorts – Walter Otton
England International Football Team Quiz & Trivia Book – George Cross

www.gate17.co.uk

Printed in Great Britain
by Amazon

74345781R00085